Growing Up Male
In America

Growing Up Male In America

Dr. M. Dean Patton

To order additional copies of this book, contact:
Xlibris Corporation
1-888-795-4274
www.Xlibris.com
Orders@Xlibris.com
34593

CONTENTS

Preface

The phrase, "growing up," is not meant to imply that any one male in America has completed his growth process no matter what age he has chronologically reached. For my purposes, "growing up" means participating in a maturing process. And in this case, the maturing process is taking place in the United States of America. What happens, and what has happened, in that maturing process to confuse males about who they are as individuals is the content of the presentation here. Probably, for about sixty years, give or take one or two years, I have participated in the "growing up" process in the U.S.A. I can't be sure about what did or did not happen to me in the first three or four years of my life, even though they were impressively formative.

Conceivably, there are some males that have not experienced the confusion about their masculinity and their roles as males that my life encompasses; and there are countless other males who have experienced this confusion. Still, no one has to admit that he has been confused. A particularly homophobic person would not want to admit any confusion. A subtle, codependent person will be masterfully skilled at denial.

The motivation for attempting to write about *Growing Up Male in America* comes from a lifelong experience of providing therapeutic counseling and teaching, and from my life experiences of confusion that I believe happened because of growing up as an American male. Why do I think that I have something to say that others have not already said? I'm not sure that I do. But I think that I do! Perhaps it is my motivation to say something about male development in a non-sterile manner, and that is not to dismiss the valuable research that has taken place already and will most likely support the intentions of this presentation. Without a doubt, woven into my motivation for writing is my own self-verification of what I know happened to me and the empathy I feel for those men whose pain of confusion immobilized them into a shelf life.

A shelf life is what the term implies, a reactive place where one waits for something to happen. As I did counseling with men of all ages and in particular older teenagers, typically college age men, especially, and more mature males (men in their 30's and 40's), I noticed something distinctly different in their attitude formation and in their perception about themselves compared with females of similar age. The males appeared to be more confused about who they were as persons compared to females of a similar age. Both males and females alike were confused, if they had been abused physically, emotionally, and/or sexually. However, men expressed more anxiety about their roles and personal image as a male. By far, many of the men suffered from approval needs. They did not get basic approval from their fathers and/or older men who played significant roles in their lives.

As a result, mothers and other females were turned to in order to fill the emotional void created by fathers, uncles, grandfathers, older brothers, and additional extended family males. This void has created other social difficulties in addition to codependency and confused identity as a male person.

My motivating purpose in presenting my observations and research is to expose the reader to information seldom talked about or even explored. It is to raise insightful questions about one's own life history or about some significant male(s) that were loved and cared about. It is to encourage discussion and exploration of what is not necessary to be a person or even a male person. It is to excite male persons to redefine who they are according to what they are—human beings, and not some codependent pattern of behavior that is deemed socially acceptable because of someone else's comfort level and someone else's expectations. I would encourage a male revolution in America. My focus is not primarily about homosexual behavior or about the Gay/Liberation Front. Nevertheless, that topic will be quite relevant from time to time in the discussion, and therefore specifically included.

The questions I am raising will hopefully find you no matter where you are as a person and/or as a male person. Perhaps, healthiness will result.

In other words, I am writing this book so that men can focus on who they are as individuals, really, and not on what others expect them to be. I want to encourage men, at least in our country, to challenge the typical stereotypes, forms, and traditional behavior patterns that society deliberately imposes on us to control us and to cage us into a limited celebration of freedom and liberty. Jesus said, "I have come to set the captives free." It is my personal desire to help men who are captivated by their dependency on others for approval and on other's determination of their personal worthiness—to be confidently FREE!

Chapter One

Is My Birthright A Gender Trap?

Like other male children, born in a patriarchal society as opposed to a matriarchal society, I had rights of inheritance. Inheritance implies a legacy of name, property, wealth, etc., and along with good fortune comes responsibility. But just how much so called responsibility do I inherit? In all probability, far more responsibility will be laid on than most any of us would have ever bargained for. The truth is that, if you are born male in America, you most likely will have to give up more than a few human rights, and when this gradually happens there will be no intelligent reason given. I remember when I was young on the farm, which was owned by my proxy aunt and uncle, telling my aunt Ruth, "I feel pain in my back or legs or somewhere." My aunt Ruth said, "Oh that's just growing pains. They will go away when you relax and fall asleep." That statement is more truthful than one might expect. The pain occurred because of too much strenuous effort during the day, and equally valid would be the pain of expectations as we got older day by day. I felt growing pains all right!

Gary Ramey, a leading expert in early childhood development in the United States, claims that who we are at three is who we are at fifteen and at thirty and at sixty. In other words, the basic core personality is formed and what happens then is a process of education and personality modification.

Research claims that the one chromosome difference between males and females causes some significant differences in behavior and chemistry (a factor that we will deal with repeatedly). Apparently, male toddlers show more aggressive behavior than female toddlers, are more competitive, are more energetic, and usually grow larger and are more muscular or stronger in stature. This is not new information, necessarily. In addition to this observation research, there also is research that claims that male infants and toddlers prefer to be held and cuddled more than do their female counter parts. What is observed happening most of the time? Male infants are thrown around like footballs and roughed up a little so they will grow up to be a man. The rough and tumble activity with the male infant and/or toddler has nothing to do with becoming a man. Becoming a man is not a guy thing at all; it is a chemical thing. The aggressive development will occur by itself.

On the other hand, if an adult wants to train and influence the aggressive potential in the male infant and toddler, that's a choice made for the child. However, when the aggressiveness (which is always an available potential) goes beyond athletic competition and military duty, and instead shows up as abusive behavior, violation of other's rights, crimes of passion, and murder, who then is responsible? We choose to be ignorant about this information and choose to do what our forefathers did who did not have this information.

In Sam Keen's wonderfully, insightful book, *Fire in the Belly*, he describes a very important influence on male infants and their perception of how they are to be in the world. The most influential force in the first years of a male's life is his MOTHER. It is at her breast and looking into her face and eyes that the male child learns the primary emotional interpretation of what is going on around him. MOTHER is the all-important influence. Mother is the source of food and the nurturer. Mother is the Interpreter of the immediate environment and the Protector, and Mother is the predominant Law Giver.[1]

Isn't it worthy of our consideration to take a look at how this major influence sets up the male infant and toddler for the rest of his life? Is it possible that mothers in America predispose their male children to a life wrought with confusion because of their aspirations for their sons? Not necessarily in an intentional way do they mean to create a malaise for male children in their ensuing years, but they believe all along that the straightjacket of expectations they are strapping them in is for their own good.

Let's take a phrase as simple as this directive that sounds like a reasonable request, "Be a good boy." Generally speaking, we know that this phrase means don't be overbearing and do what you are told and what is expected of you.

On the other hand, what the hell does, "Be a good boy," mean? I think most likely, at an early toddler age, it feels like a subtle form of intimidation. When the same phrase is less subtle, it may sound like this: "I'm warning you, you had better be a good boy or else!" What does the else mean? You can be sure that between three and four years of age the male child knows what it means for him. Is the meaning consistent? No! It can be argued that the same is true for female children as well. This is true, but for our purposes the focus is on the male child. It is probably safe to say that the male child is more clear and less confused about what is negative about him and his behavior than he may ever be about what is positive about him and his behavior.

At the same time a male infant/toddler is expected to wade through a mirage of subtle expectations, he must begin to understand gender expectations. More frequently than not, when the male infant/toddler begins to discover his body, he is discouraged from this behavior with the quick, convenient response—that's dirty or nasty. If he is going to discover much about his gender physically, he most likely will do it in a closeted way. Why? Because he is shamed! Who does the shaming? Most likely, the Mother. Since when does a female know what it is like to have her genitalia exposed? Who is more likely to influence the male infant/toddler's attitude formation about his penis? That's correct—the mother.

Now in conjunction with this discovery of exposed genitalia, the male infant/toddler realizes that he is vulnerable. He is not vulnerable because he may fall down the stairs or off the bed or dart out into the street or crawl off the end of the porch. He is vulnerable because there is this giant male called "dad" around the house. Sometimes he changes diapers and sometimes he gives the bath. Sometimes mommy does not protect or rescue, instead she asks daddy to take over because she is frustrated. Is it possible that daddies would take away their son's penis and testicles? When daddy is angry with mommy and she with him, who knows what he might do. Most male toddlers are left to come to some acceptable resolve on their own. This is one of the first and most significant transitions for a male toddler. It has been my experience that this a situation taken humorously by parents. Many mothers are too embarrassed to talk about the fact that their son wants to marry them. Eventually the male toddler may discover that his father can be his friend and maybe the initial bonding (if the process took place) can be renewed. It is a period in which basic approval can be given and/or offered. Although, most of the men I have counseled or mentored do not remember such bonding or support. So much for Freud's theory of "Psychological [Sociological] Dynamics of Child Development."

Since ninety percent of the men in this country have learned, by their late teens, what they believe is socially acceptable in the role of father, very few have opportunity to explore this role and to practically apply what they think they know. Male toddlers, and little boys to seven or eight year olds, almost automatically are attracted to baby dolls. In most situations with which I am familiar, toddlers and little boys are prevented from playing with dolls. Sometimes the discouragement is subtle and sometimes it is quite intimidating. If you play with baby dolls, you'll grow up to be a "sissy." Unless a male child gets some early practice and/or gets some actual child care practice (baby-sitting) experience, he will be literally frightened and ignorant in providing childcare for his own kids. This is another envelope of confusion.

Parents are rather reluctant to explain why it is not good to play with baby dolls and it is not good to play house and/or hospital with little girls. I remember a time in my early childhood when a very similar situation occurred. Around the age of five, there were more little girls in my block than there were little boys other than my brother, who was two years older and did not prefer to play with me, if given a choice. At age seven, he was allowed across the busy, city street while I was not. During my fourth and fifth years, therefore, my daily companions were little girls. I would play house, and I would be the daddy who was supposed to mimic the little girl's father in behavior or my own father's behavior. Some days instead of playing house we would play hospital or school. Those of us who had older siblings would mimic them when we played school. But, when we played house and hospital, the scene inevitably changed to more domestic and intimate circumstances. Understandably, then, the little girls and I would go to bed and mimic our parents or what we thought they did in bed. Eventually, because we repeated these pretend bedroom scenes or hospital scenes, off came our clothes, and we became more and more exploratory in our touching and seeing. It was innocent enough; however, our parents didn't think so.

My parents appeared to be less aware than the parents of the little girls. One late afternoon, a group of the parents of the little girls came to our residence and confronted my parents with my sexual behavior. At that time, I didn't know enough to call my behavior sexual or even what sex was. What I did know was that my genitalia were different from my little girl friends. Collectively, all the parents joined together in condemning my behavior and believed that if I were not prevented from playing with the little girls I would turn into a rapist. As a result, my second encounter with the meaning of my genitalia was that my penis and testicles had to be covered at all times except, of course, when I went to the bathroom and when I took a bath. Allowing little girls to touch my genitalia was forbidden and I was forbidden to touch their crouch and breasts. This was a very bad thing to do, and I was never to do it again. In addition, my father, usually a reasonable and supporting person, mounted a campaign against my playing with little girls by naming that activity as being "sissy." My brother's two years of development and experience beyond me was also programmed into the campaign so I wouldn't become a sissy. My mother and sister accepted my father's efforts and at any opportunity reminded me not to be a sissy.

I remember this brief period of playing house as the beginning of my training for the responsibilities of being a father. Comparatively speaking, I am aware of how many diapers I have changed as an adult male and how few diapers other males I have known changed. I remember how many infants I watched from the time I was ten or eleven years old, and how few other boys were trusted with this responsibility. My pretending to be a father helped me to learn a father's role compared with little boys who never played house and mimicked the father's behavior.

At this period of time in my life, when I felt unacceptable because I was told I was being a sissy and a bad boy, a male influence emerged who was a loving, positive, wonderful, spirited person. He was my maternal grandfather, who was father of nine children. My grandmother died the year I was born, and he had come to live with us. I cannot begin to imagine how much confusion he rescued me from. It is not that my parents were not great and wonderful people, they certainly were. However, like other households, the family was dysfunctional, and they, after all, were part of American society.

After a long wait to the age of six in May, 1946, it was hard for me to believe that I would start school in the fall. I was prepared to go to the first grade. In addition to knowing how to tie my shoes, and how to recognize my colors, and say my alphabet, I could add and subtract. I was also well indoctrinated with a mess of contradictions in my head. One of the first things I knew was that I was bad. I heard that more often than I was good. It was bad to touch my genitalia or let little girls touch me there. I was bad because I liked being touched. I was not good enough because I played with little girls and that turned me into a sissy. I was better off not to have anything to do with girls. I should play with boys and develop my muscles. I should do more because I was big for my age.

No one said anything when adult males fondled me. On occasion, during holiday seasons, I would have to sleep with an uncle. There were two different uncles who touched me and would rub their penis on my legs. One of them would hold me close to him and we would play "chair." That meant he would eventually work his erection between my legs and let it remain there for most of the night. I told my father about some of it when I was in college. Why didn't I say something sooner? Because I was bad, and it was bad and dirty to have anything to do with genitalia. Adult males were good but not me. Even though I had blonde curls on my head, a well-structured physique, and a handsome face, I was a bad boy on the inside and soon to be an inferior weakling.

Is my male gender a birthright trap? Yes! When I consider the United Nations charter of Human Rights and/or the first 10 Amendments to the United States Constitution, which is our Bill of Rights, I may be making the presumption that most men realize that their rights are being eroded away by cultural translation. We are promised freedom, dignity, and equality under the law. We are promised that we can pursue life, liberty, and happiness. These statements of human rights translate into the promise that we can live securely without discrimination regarding race, color, sex, language, religious, political, or other opinions, national or social origin, property, birth or other status. Some examples of the erosion of our rights as men follow:

Men who are smaller and weaker—Dominated by the larger, stronger
Men who are shy and reserved—Spoken for by others more bold
Men who are not as committed—Responded to as burdensome
Men who object to war and killing—Regarded as unpatriotic cowards
Men who express emotions publicly—Perhaps more effeminate
Men in a career dominated by women—Questionable masculinity
Men of color—Subversive minorities corrupting American culture
Men born on the wrong side of the tracks—Future prisoners/convicts
Men who choose a male spouse—Sick, queer ass, weirdo
Men who choose bachelorhood—Odd and possibly a closet queen
Men who use their cerebral potential—Geeks, inept athletes, nerds
Men who have different political views—Un-American troublemaker
Men who do not compete aggressively—A wimpy waste as a male

Damn it!

I have the right to my own thoughts and beliefs
I have the right to say "No!"
I have the right to do with my body as I wish
I have the right to exercise my liberty within the law

I have the right to give what I choose
I have the right to receive what I choose
I have the right to be critical of our culture
I have the right to criticize our government

What is happening and has happened to our personal rights as an American person, who is born male?

Chapter Two

The Hurting Boy, Inside

We are quite adept, in this country, of making sure that we rear our male children to be red blooded, all American boys. There are a number of different interpretations of what this means. Collectively, however, there are a number of traits or characteristics that are to be encouraged. The "you-have-to-be's" list is not exhaustive or inclusive, but relates the most common aspirations adult guardians have for those male children in their care:

"Big boys don't show their feelings,"
"Big boys can take or endure pain,"
"Big boys are brave,"
"Big boys are strong,"
"Big boys are aggressive,"
"Big boys are persistent,"
"Big boys are mischievous,"
"Big boys are promiscuous,"
"Big boys take advantage of opportunities,"
"Big boys are athletic,"
"Big boys are manly,"
"Big boys are dominating."

The list goes on, but these characteristics are the predominating ones that prove a boy is being properly trained to be a red-blooded all-American male. And if a young male demonstrates most of the listed characteristics and wants to still play with a baby doll—then what? And, if young men demonstrate most of these characteristics, but have special God given talents to be excellent cooks, interior decorators, colorful artists in both the fine and performing arts, does this somehow reflect negatively upon their genetic ability to be a respected person, a man's man? While it makes no sense logically, biologically, psychologically, socially, and morally, it appears more frequently than not that men who embody the "Big boy characteristics," and extend into talents that are identified as feminine are immediately suspect.

I remember being in my later twenties living in a suburb of Buffalo, New York, as a Presbyterian Minister, when I became more aware of this strange phenomenon. A young man, who was a golden gloves champion, was a successful barber. I found out quite by accident, that he was very skillful at hair design for women. I asked why he didn't let the public know more about his talent as a hairdresser? His response was, "Surely you know what men would think of me if I did. I'd be considered light in my loafers." I immediately knew what he meant because we both had attended similar schools in our culture where we were carefully taught. I told him that if I were a golden gloves champion, I wouldn't worry about it. When I had the chance, I kept encouraging him. Eventually, he increased his economic circumstances significantly as a very successful hair designer.

Although I didn't know it, the point of view expressed by my barber friend had already been instilled in me by age six. When it comes to our experiences of our transformation, that begin with entry into elementary school, parents are often unaware of the effects upon us (their sons). Even at this moment of innocence, we begin to realize this pushing, patterned force which defines what we can or can not feel or express.

First grade was a real transition for me. If I was going to be respected, I was sure I had to believe in my father's campaign hook, line, and sinker. I said good-bye to baby dolls, lead soldiers, playing house, and began to practice being male. It was so important to me to be accepted and approved of that I quickly overdid it. Other than with my older brother, I really had no experience fighting and certainly no experience street fighting. At first I was intimidated by most of the other males who became my playmates. I had not yet understood that I, or any all-American male child, had to defend myself and I had to be tough enough to intimidate others to not mess around with me. I learned that winning a fistfight was a show of strength and dominance.

As I said, I did come on a little strong, and my first grade teacher was not going to put up with it. I was very competitive. My older sister and brother were strong personalities, as are most persons in my family, and I had learned to compete with them for my mother's attention shortly after I was born. Noon recess in the schoolyard and periods of time before school began and ended were perfect times to practice my competitive, aggressive skills. I was just being a boy right? Ms. R_____, a flaming redhead, would frequently open our classroom window to scream threats of discipline at me. I talked out of turn too much, and when my classroom work was completed, I was constantly out of my seat. She was forever giving me extra work to do or giving me tasks to do, i.e. erasing the chalk boards, dusting the erasers, taking a note to another teacher in the square, two floor, four classroom elementary building. The paddle which hung on the wall underneath the clock was often removed to be used on me. To be honest, the paddle would be used once or twice a week on me and sometimes twice a day. I was being aggressive, dominant, and learning to guard my feelings. I would not cry, especially not when she paddled me in front of the class. The little girls I used to play with disliked me because I was often the reason why the whole class had to stay after school was officially over as a means of discipline. My playmates and/or cronies admired my bravery and approved of my ability to take the beating without showing my feelings.

Now I realize that part of my difficulty was that I was ADD—Attention Deficit Disorder. I was somewhat hyper and was slightly deficit in self-control. The world was recovering from WWII, when I began school, and no one cared about doing ADD research. Actually it was not until the 80's that this terminology was incorporated into our educational and medical language. To make matters worse, in some ways, for every one around including me, was the fact that I was "gifted and talented." Very few persons of authority in education, if any, were aware of the breadth of intelligence and the variety of skill and talent that was possible in a child. It would take a few decades and a great deal of psychological research before the concept of the gifted and talented would be verified and recognized. What does it feel like to be gifted and talented in a world that does not approve and/or understand? Totally frustrating and most of the time rather lonely.

Generally, my perception of my immediate environment is very acute, and my understanding about the meaning of situations and/or circumstances is quick. Cognitively, I am an associative and differential processor, more than I am a magnitude thinker. Without getting into a lengthy explanation, I am considered a creative thinker. I am a very visual person who is balanced with verbal and tactile cognitive processes. This means, if I am interested, I grasp information quickly and process its relevance immediately. A basic motivation, that probably began before I was born, was a need to know. Broad interests and curiosity, in addition to quick perceptive skills, complicated by creative ability, nearly drove adults, who were around me, insane. I understand that under the circumstances they did the best they could do, but they were also cruel. Adults who did not understand how or why I was different treated me as an overbearing brat. I had a big mouth and was considered to be a smart ass. In the classroom, I was considered by most teachers to be a constant irritant. What did it feel like to be me as a first grader? Like I didn't quite fit in anywhere. I was told that I was bad for exploring my human sexual anatomy, that I was bad for playing with little girls, that I was bad because I could potentially be a sissy, that I was bad for eventually turning into a neighborhood bully, and that I was bad because I thought I knew too much. Was I rewarded for being the top reader in my class? No! I was told and warned that I should not get too big for my britches! Ms. R_____ told my first grade class that even though I had some of the best grades in the class, I failed in deportment and may end up repeating first grade.

Thank God for grandfathers like my maternal grandfather! He always told me what the rules were and he would always set me down and calm me down. He accepted me and confirmed me, and, most importantly, he hugged me. He would explain away a significant amount of confusion. He didn't run to get the bar of soap when I used vulgar language. He explained the meaning of what I was saying because he knew I would make a different choice of expression. I remember being angry with my brother and I called him a bastard. My grandfather took me into the bathroom and sat me down on the edge of the bathtub and explained what the word *bastard* meant. In the meantime my brother went to tell my mother, who was now pounding on the bathroom door. My grandfather calmly said, "I'm taking care of the situation." Even today, I seldom, if ever, use the word. I had learned that a rooster was also called a cock. For a very brief period of time, I went around calling people, who were my age, a "cock head." It was my grandfather who taught me about the double meaning of words.

Another thing my grandfather taught me about was *mystification*. Mystification, as John Bradshaw describes it in his book, *Homecoming*, happens when a child knows what he has seen and heard, but an adult tries to contradict the child's observation and conclusion. The phrase, "Oh no, that's what you think you heard or what you think you saw," is an expression of mystification. My grandfather appreciated the gift of my imagination, but when he wanted the truth, I had better not fabricate. I would object because others, and especially adults, told stories that were not true, why couldn't I? He explained the meaning of gossip and mystification and why these behaviors could be so destructive. I have related these life lessons and relied heavily upon John Bradshaw's concept/description of how a child becomes wounded through "mystification" because this subtle way of fabrication confuses a child. As a child, I grew up thinking that most everything adults said or did was a contradiction. I was learning that contradictions were the real truth, which adults energetically defended. A quick example is: A child does something that adults consider funny and everyone laughs. The next day a child does the same thing, but a parent says, "You do that again and I'll slap you." Is this a description of what is referred to as a contradiction? Do contradictions cause confusion?

Chapter 3

Removing the Cellophane

Going to school, having had no preparation except for what was accomplished at home, was my first transformative experience. When I was a kid, cellophane was a clear covering put on special gifts or items that were new. It was a lot like plastic wrap except it was more rigid and not readily available for home use. A person could gently remove the cellophane or tear it up as he or she removed this transparent covering from the new item. I felt like I was covered in cellophane, when I went to school for the first time. I remember my cellophane being ripped off! It was frightening and painful and I would never be the same again. I, like many males my age in America, was entering the world of independent training. It would mean that each and every male (and girls too) would be engaged in some form of testing to prove we could think and act in an independent manner. The list of the "To be's," just got significantly longer.

Our entire public educational system was and is based on competition and peer pressure, which is a major factor in motivating our kids to achieve academically and athletically. Rather than concentrating on the development of intrinsic motivation, grade school males were taught that they had to be right when they volunteered an answer. If one were wrong too many times, he would be called on less and less and would be told that he was wrong and would soon come to understand that as he failed other classmates were succeeding. Use of imagination was a reward more than being an intrinsic ingredient of the lesson plan. "You know what children, if each and everyone of you behaves as a class, we will do some art this afternoon," we were told by the teacher. And she would look at me scornfully to make sure that I knew that I was not to screw up. I recall making little Easter Baskets to take home to our mothers. I don't recall ever making anything to take home to our fathers. Perhaps the teacher really didn't like men? Anyway, I knew nothing about that at the time and went on to make my basket. It was a pattern that the teacher had prepared and if the pupils followed instructions, cutting the art paper and folding it correctly, it would become a little basket. The teacher would supply the manufactured straw and jelly beans. Before I cut my basket out, I drew little squares of equal size on what would be the basket part and alternately colored the squares purple and yellow. I drew some flowers and colored them to place at the juncture where the handle and basket would connect.

The teacher yelled at me, "You just had to be different didn't you. Do I have to watch you every minute so that you do what you are told?" So much for imagination, creativity, and ADHD. This is part of the content of the first major transformation or actual change in my life, and I suspect some of the meaning of this content is similar to most young males in America. Most males in 1946 did not have the advantage of Head Start Programs or kindergarten or nursery school before being taken into the institution of public education. This transformation took me away from my grandfather, and my parents, and my familiar surroundings, and where the learning process happened as life happened. I was aware that I was a boy, which didn't mean much other than I looked like my brother and dad and grandfather. And, I believed that I was taken care of and loved. Nevertheless, I got the distinct feeling that nobody really cared about me and what I needed and wanted. Most people cared about what they got from me including the teacher(s). In those days teachers, who could be ill-prepared tyrants, were utterly respected. If there was misbehavior at school, there would be hell to pay at home. Reflectively, I think I felt abandoned. All too soon I was expected to fit into the pattern of national need. I had to be assimilated into society one way or another, and I had to pass tests in order to prove that the teacher was doing her job. Even though my test grades were high, I was not recognized favorably at school.

Perhaps by now, a reader may begin to think that my explanations are a pity party. To a degree that may be true, but there were no alternatives to being forced into the Teddy Roosevelt model of the American male. If a male kid didn't fit or conform, he would eventually become more and more of a victim. He would be pushed aside if he were not an extrovert, an athlete, and somewhat of a daredevil. If a male was introverted, intuitive, sensitive, and artistic, he did not fit into the self-made man image or model.[1] If the young, impressionable, elementary school male was a budding bully, extroverted, mischievous, egocentric, capable athletically, and was also sensitive, intuitive, and artistic, he was somewhat suspect and considered to be weird and kept on the periphery of his gang of friends. How does it feel to be someone like this? It feels awfully damn lonely. Nevertheless, as I look back, most of my cronies and my older brother and I were being indoctrinated with the characteristics of the self-made man. Teddy Roosevelt and his "Rough Riders" were heroic to my father.

Growing up to be a "self-made man" was a continuing theme on the farm where I would frequently escape. Because I had a well-established relationship with my extended family, (Aunt Ruth and Uncle Bill by proxy), who were neighbors when I was an infant and toddler, and now owned and lived on a farm. I would call on a Friday and ask my Aunt Ruth or Uncle Bill to come and get me, and they very rarely were unable to make arrangements to accommodate me. Fortunately for me, Uncle Bill and Aunt Ruth were very loving and supportive in their participation of my rearing and education. Many weekends and summers were primarily spent on the farm. School days were spent with my family in the city. Unless circumstances prevented me from being on the farm, I was there learning and helping, and sometimes getting into trouble. It was only after becoming an adult that I realized how devoted to me that they were. Most kids growing up on a farm know how fast a male child (as well as a female child) must learn because another pair of hands, particularly if the hands are skilled, can be very helpful.

I suppose nearly every mother and father dread the time when their children begin to understand how they got into their mother's belly, and how they get out of there. In my generation, young males often appeared to be deprived of information that females were privileged to know. I had access to information that many city dwelling males did not. A significant dimension of information that influenced my transformation was the sexual behavior of the typical farm animals. As I watched what happened between cows and bulls, stallions and mares, boars and sows, roosters and hens, it didn't take long for me to figure out that intercourse had something to do with procreation. By questioning Aunt Ruth and especially Uncle Bill, I was putting information together rather quickly. Of course, my conclusions were always checked out with my most trusted friend, my grandfather. As a

six year old on the farm, helpful skills began to be developed. My training
to milk cows began. Hoeing the tender plants in a huge vegetable garden,
running a power mower, picking fruits, and helping with the harvest of
crops and the harvest of the vegetable garden taught me what hard work is.
Helping to feed and water the animals among many other tasks was also an
education. Being held responsible and accountable was an understanding
that came along with the benefits of being at the farm. Uncle Bill, in
addition, to being a farmer was also a contractor/carpenter, who built homes
and whatever else that could be crafted from wood. He was a man's man,
and it was obvious that he wouldn't agree or submit to anything that he did
not believe in. He was aggressive as well as kind and sensitive at times. He
contributed a lot of knowledge to my emotional memory, knowledge about
being masculine. It could be said that while I was on the farm, Uncle Bill
perpetrated masculinity. There were tasks and feats to perform and achieve,
and all the while he knew that I was struggling to prove that I was equal
to the challenge, he never laughed at me. At home in the city, it seemed to
me that everyone, except my grandfather, was perpetrating masculinity, and
especially in the Teddy Roosevelt image. What does it mean to perpetrate
masculinity?

Terrence Real, author of *I Don't Want to Talk about It*, is a critical research
source. He has been doing research in male depression and he explains, for
decades, feminist scholars and social researchers have patiently built up a
body of evidence showing the psychological damage done by the coercive
enforcement of gender roles in girls. But what about the damage to the
psychological development of boys? If traditional socialization takes aim at
girls' voices, it takes aim at boys' hearts. Little boys and little girls start off
with similar psychological profiles. They are equally emotional, expressive,
and dependent, equally desirous of physical affection. At the youngest ages,
both boys and girls are more like a stereotypical girl. If any differences exist,
little boys are, in fact, slightly more sensitive and expressive than little girls.
They cry more easily, seem more easily frustrated, appear more upset when
a caregiver leaves the room. Until the age of four or five, both boys and girls
rest comfortably in what one researcher has called "the expressive-affiliate
mode." Studies indicate that girls are permitted to remain in that mode while
boys are subtly—or forcibly—pushed out of it.[2]

To add to the explanation of masculine perpetration, an Australian
anthropologist, Bob Connell writes that, "Agencies of socialization cannot
produce mechanical effects in a growing person." What they do is invite the

[male] child to participate in social practice on given terms. The invitation may be, and often is, coercive—accompanied by heavy pressure to and no mention of an alternative. "Mama's boy," "fagot," "pussy," "wimp"—no boy I know of has escaped the experience of such ridicule. No man I have treated has fully eluded the taste of the lash one receives if one dares not accept masculinity's "invitation." [3]

I remember one of my father's favorite ways of disciplining me for talking back to my mother, and that was to sneak up behind me and smack the back of my head. In the moments immediately afterwards, I remember feeling a hateful rage. Momentarily, I hated my father. The hateful rage I felt did not accomplish what my father had intended. It did not make me increase my respect for my mother! Instead, that adult male behavior taught me to never turn my back on any one of my gender. It taught me not to trust my father's judgment or choices, and it taught me still another way a person could be belittled and/or diminished. Even today, I choose to feel insulted and angry when some male decides to touch my bald head, especially when I am sitting down. When my father would rap me on the back of the head, I felt violated. The emotion was the same as when I felt like the cellophane had been ripped off of me.

On the farm, "I can't" was not acceptable as a response. Saying "I can't" did not necessarily mean "I won't." Sometimes the request or demand would be beyond what a growing boy had the capacity to accomplish, although a mature male could. If I complained of difficulty, I was given examples of men I knew, but did not respect. These men were wimps. And, I would be asked, "Do you want to be thought of as one those guys?" I would be told, "Don't whine! If you need help, ask me for help, just don't whine!" Although there is merit in this teaching response, there were alternative ways of teaching the same lesson without putting others down in the process or threatening that I would have the same image. But, then, another way may not be likely to perpetrate masculinity.

I recall being about six or seven, when my older sister, who was seven years older than I, compared my biceps to those of my older brother, who was two years older. I was told that my brother's muscles were hard and mine were like a bag of sand. This is another example of how masculinity is perpetuated. She really impacted me, and, by the time I was eight or nine, I had developed biceps like rocks. Working on the farm helped a great deal.

Equally important to developing muscles, all-American boys have to acquire a certain amount of sexual information. I have called it information because it does not necessarily mean it is factual, and usually it is not. Men in my generation and those that follow have rarely been accurately prepared with correct information about their anatomy/physiology and the anatomy/physiology of females. And the attitude that gets transmitted along with inaccurate information is that they are the pursuers, the dominant force, and the seducing penetrator. Females are expected to be submissive. Learning about sex behind the barn or behind the garage or behind some cover, immediately suggests that sex is dirty, something to be hidden, something that causes guilt, and you are bad if you participate in it.

One day in the elementary school yard, I was flashing a jack knife or a penknife around. A kid I wasn't allowed to associate with, and who used to bully me around in the neighborhood until one afternoon when I pounded him into the ground, came up to me wanting to make a trade. (If my dad knew that I had a knife, he would have been furious. He had been in a fight and was stabbed.) The kid had a deck of playing cards, but they were not actually playing cards. The deck had fifty-two XXXXX rated pictures of every imaginable act. The pictures revealed heterosexual activity as well as homosexual activity. After school a considerable number of boys followed me home. We formed a circle behind the garage and I began circulating the pictures around the group. Some of the boys wanted to borrow a few of the cards overnight and so I said okay. A neighbor saw that we were passing cards to one another, but did not know what game we were playing. She reported it to my parents. After dinner the phone started ringing. It was the parents of some of the boys who took the "dirty" cards home. They were in a rage! I have to give my father credit; he stayed calm and told these parents he would look into the matter and take care of it. He sat me down alone and looking straight into my eyes asked me about the deck of cards. I told him that most of these cards were in my possession and how I had come to have them. He demanded that I give the deck to him immediately, and straight away I went to my bedroom where my brother was busy looking at them. Shortly the notorious deck was in my father's hands. He told me that we were, in the very near future, going to sit down and talk about sex. That talk never happened. Some of the boys tried to give me back some of the pictures they had borrowed right in the classroom. I was terrified that the teacher would catch us. She did. Ms. R_____ went ballistic. She called my father to come to the school immediately. (Something he would have to do frequently because of my brother's or my misbehavior.) My dad came and calmed my teacher down, in the back room, while he glowered at me. He was humiliated! Apparently, I was no longer the darling sissy.

Terrence Real, author of *I Don't Want to Talk about It,* quotes the following from the father in *Prince of Tides,*

> I do not take shit from women. [he tells his wife] You're a woman and nothing but a goddamn woman and keep your goddamn mouth shut when I'm disciplining one of the boys. I do not interfere with you and Savannah because I do not give a shit how you raise her. But it's important to raise a boy up right. Because there's nothing worse on earth than a boy who ain't been *brought up right.*[4]

Real follows with this comment,

> For more than one might care to imagine, being "brought up right," means active trauma. But even boys who begin in a nonviolent atmosphere may find the enforcement of the masculine role ratcheting up if they dare try stepping outside of it.[5]

The more research I do the more I am convinced that physical and emotional abuse of American males, in some of the most subtle ways, is the acceptable way of rearing boys by father and *mother!* Terrence Real says, "Some boys lose their "souls" in great chunks, others find it chipped away in small bits, through the most ordinary interactions,"[6] One of the significant ways that my brother and I found out about the masculinity mold was by being pinned against one another in brutal competition. As wise as my father was, he made a very tragic mistake. He played my brother and me against one another by the time we were in grade school. The cellophane was completely removed, and some depression was beginning to be experienced.

Chapter 4

Outside In and Inside Out

E li H. Newberger, M.D. author of *The Men They Will Become*, writes the following as he attempts to begin to define character development in male children.

We wouldn't have any way of discerning character if it weren't tested by hard circumstances. The testing often comes from outside as a challenge. It can also come from inside as a boy deliberately tests his own limits. But where does character come from in the first place? . . . . At the beginning of his life, a boy scarcely has a self. He has a temperament, which I shall discuss later, but not a character. His world is microcosmic—consisting of himself and the people who take care of him. His strongest social instinct is to bond very closely to his mother. Very quickly he experiences tension between what he wants and what he is being given. In the course of infancy and early childhood, every one of his desires will be tested. . . . . Depending on how he is treated, an infant boy develops fundamental attitudes about himself and his surroundings. He may develop a capacity for intimacy because he is held and stroked and talked to lovingly a lot; or he may become accustomed to detachment from others because his first principal caregivers were somewhat distant toward him. [1]

Eli Newberger has presented information that is very important to the overall point of view of this book. For a number of years, I would try to teach college freshmen and sophomores about this insight. In other words, I would encourage the students to understand that their sense of their internal life comes about, in a significant way, through information encountered and absorbed from their environment. We can distinguish this information as the "Internal Map," which we carry around with us all of our lives. The internal map depends on perceptions of information that is absorbed through the five senses, and the emotional memory. The process of building the internal map most likely gets initiated in the womb. The map is formed and functional by age three. It can be changed or altered only by consistent evidence that change is necessary, but there is no guarantee that it will. The "External Map", on the other hand, functions as our navigational guide in society and assists in the process of assimilation of our public culture and our family culture. Modification of the external map occurs when the pressures and circumstances of the environment demand it. Perhaps, this is an alternative way of explaining the methodical development of human character. Eli Newberger, in his explanation of character says:

> Responsible parents begin to give their children structure and guidelines early in life so that the building blocks for resiliency, strength, and respect for others are laid. In other words, the building blocks of character. The only way to tell what a boy is absorbing from his tutelage is to observe how he behaves, particularly in a situation where there is some tension that pulls him between alternative choices.[2]

Newberger concludes that:

> "Character thus consists of a constantly evolving balance between a boy's inner desires and ideals and the forces of his environment. The balance can shift in an instant."

James Comer, a psychiatrist at Yale, is quoted by Newberger as saying,

> When I grew up, there was a conspiracy of adults to make me a
> responsible person.' And there is not that conspiracy today, or
> at least it's weakened. So [male] kid's decisions are based on the
> influences of popular culture and peer influences more than they
> are on the adult voice.[3]

Since Newberger believes that character and temperament development
are an interactive dynamic. It is necessary to complete the whole picture
of his concept about character and temperament. Newberger says, "Every
boy is born with an innate temperament and other inherited characteristics
that will be his for a lifetime, and that influences the way he behaves in any
situation."

It is the research of Chess and Thomas that Newberger calls upon to
describe the nine irreducible components of temperament:

1   Activity Level. How intense is his activity, and what is the proportion
    of active to inactive periods in his day?
2. Regularity. How predictable or unpredictable is he in the timing of
    basic biological functions such as eating and sleeping?
3. Approach or Withdrawal. How does he react initially to new situations?
4. Adaptability. How does he respond over time to new or altered
    situations?
5. Sensory Threshold. How much stimulus does he need before he
    responds?
6. Mood. How pleasant and friendly, or unfriendly, is he?
7. Intensity of Reaction. How energetic is his response, positively or
    negatively?
8. Distractibility. How easily does a new stimulus interfere with ongoing
    activity?
9. Persistence and Attention Span. Does he continue activities in the face of
    obstacles? How long will he pursue an activity before abandoning it?[4]

Newberger, finally, concludes that:

> Temperament and character each affect the other. Temperament
> influences how receptive the [male] child will be to life experiences,

and how life experiences will be absorbed by the child. Character, as it develops over the years, becomes a resource for shaping the part of temperament that is malleable."[5]

In other words, once male children are brained washed and duped into the cultural definition of what masculinity is, it will be difficult to modify this belief and behavior.

Although there may be further debates or further discussions on the formation of character and temperament and how the dynamic of interaction between a man's environment and himself influences him, there is not enough space, at this time, to carry forth with this particular deliberation. The point of reporting this research is to establish when and how American males slowly develop the characters and emotional expression that they pay for most of their lives.

From the ages of seven or eight to eleven or twelve the definitive behavior of what a male must do to become a real man gets quite clear. At the same time it is confusing and contradictory at best. For most American boys the "latency" period has moved in on them, and they are more interested in sports and outdoor games and heroes. At least for me, anything sexual was momentary, I didn't have much to do with girls because they had to be taken care of and took up too much time. If I even thought about more than gender difference, it was because an adult, primarily males, were putting a move on me. It didn't matter where we seemed to be, what mattered was we were alone together and somewhat private. I suppose I was perceived as being vulnerable and naive. The situation never seemed to enable them to take advantage of me. Either someone came upon us or something would occur and I had an opportunity to escape. Of course I knew that I felt uncomfortable in those situations, and I thought I was acting silly because all of these men were very familiar to me and some I would see every week. I wasn't reared to understand or accept affection from men.

I have a very good, long term memory. By the way, I did get to the second grade with my classmates even though Ms. R_____ had threatened me with failing deportment. Ms. N_____ had just gotten married, and she was a nicer person than that Ms. R_____. Ms. N_____ would talk to me and tell me what she expected of me. When she reasoned with me, it made sense, which proved to me that I wasn't as obstinate as I was made out to be. She avoided invoking and/or perpetuating the masculine behavior model in me. We had some ADHD misunderstandings, but I was never paddled, and there were few times that I had to stand in the corner or sit in the back of the room. Nevertheless, I continued to have excellent grades and my only competition was from one of the girls in the class. She was black but that didn't matter; I was sweet on her and she liked me.

It was during this period of time that I realized that the youngest of my mother's five brothers was an alcoholic. I didn't understand addiction, and I didn't understand the shunning shame of it all. Uncle Norman, before going to World War II, had been a different man. He was a tall, handsome, very talented, and skilled person. When he came home from the war, Uncle Norman was addicted to cigarettes, alcohol, and sex. His bisexuality was kept a secret. I was never told until I was an older teenager. Ironically, the very one who you might expect to make a move on me didn't. The very uncles who would never have been suspected are the ones who did.

Uncle Norman during my grade school years appeared to me to be the personification of the confusion and contradiction of males growing up in America. He was someone that I studied because, when he drank, he became brave enough to tell his perspective about the family to the entire community. He was also very vulgar in his expressions. After I got over my fear of his loud voice and his vulgarity when he was drunk, I would bury my head in my pillow and laugh my ass off! The truth of the matter is that my Uncle Norman was a binge alcoholic. As a Certified Addictions Counselor (etc.), I now know what that means. I doubt very seriously if my family and the population of the USA even had this research at this time. My family, who admittedly did not know how to deal with this clinical problem, were his enablers. He did not fit the very proud family image. He was an embarrassment! But he was a red-blooded American male, wasn't he? My other uncles (most of them) at one time or another in the years I was in elementary and grade school got drunk or, at least, functionally drunk. Some of them smoked, and I personally know that some of them were apparently broader in their sexual orientation than strict heterosexuality. And yet, over and over again, my Uncle Norman would be ostracized for the same behavior, and I can only conclude that it was because he was threatening, non-compliant, and verbose. However, when Uncle Norman was sober, he was praised for his interior decorating ability, his ability and skill, and his endurance on a project. I noticed that he was not often complimented for his compassionate personality and his willingness to be helpful and nurturing. He was brave, he was a masculine man, but he was a man who broke with the silent mold that we are all aware of. He dared, when intoxicated, to tell it like it was. He dared to tell how he was forced into a mold that didn't fit his amazingly talented personhood. He absorbed his environment and he assimilated his social environment, but not quite well enough. My best guess is that he was a gifted and talented person. I also guess that he was also ADHD, who was unacceptable to a middle of the road family that contributed impactfully to the local community. Uncle Norman could internalize the map from his environment, but when he started to assimilate the map, he could not accept the contradictions or represent them publicly as though the information were valid. I had a personal and private hero, who received no help for his condition, and very little love from his embarrassed family. Only when he was resourceful and helpful, did he get civil notice and some measure of acceptance. I learned through my grade school years not to be like my Uncle Norman, who died in a motel fire, when I was sixteen years old.

Ms. H_____, my third grade teacher, was an abomination to education. She was a vicious tyrant in the classroom, and particularly hostile toward boys. Even though she had been administratively warned, it would not be long before she would be right back at the boys, pounding the boys' heads on the desk and tearing up their work. If I learned anything, I do not know how or why. Like some of my uncles, Ms. H_____ taught me not to trust adults regardless of their positions, titles, or professional responsibilities. This experience was the external message that was internalized. Too many adults played the power game, "Now I've Got You, You Little Son of a Bitch." It's the same power game as, "Just wait till the next time," or "Wait till your dad gets home."

Perhaps, the redemption of my elementary education, as the bullies of the schoolyard volleyed for position, was Ms. J_____, my fourth grade teacher. When she decided she had had enough from me early in the fall, she kept me after school and talked to me. She went to the same church as my parents and my family. She knew my parents and really respected my father, who she believed was a dedicated public leader of the community. Ms. J_____ appealed to my sense of family pride and my sense of personal importance because of who I was. ""You were born into a family that affords you an opportunity to influence hundreds and possibly thousands of people. Your importance is far beyond this small schoolyard. Being one of the top rulers of the schoolyard isn't important. Do you understand that this may be the only place some of your friends will ever sense what the top is about. You, however, will achieve and accomplish much more than this." Thank you, Ms. J_____ . Did you notice that you had no trouble from me for the rest of the year?

In this chapter I wanted to point out that male children are forced into the masculine mold by willful adult coercion, if necessary. Even though masculinity, an unclearly defined concept in our culture, is regarded as a sacred value, its ambiguity and resulting confusion pass on damaging consequences.

Chapter 5

Impactful Incidents:

Passing Tests Isn't Just Academic

I cannot leave this latent period of my life without mentioning some incidents of impact and influence on my internal and external life map. The final kiss off from elementary school happened after school on the way home. 13th Street ran through a railroad tunnel. It was constructed of large, quarried brownstone and had rough chiseled edges on the surfaces. I was late, and just as I was about to turn into a vacant lot off 13th Street, I saw a lot of commotion at the railroad tunnel. Some of my classmates, from the other side of the tracks, had someone surrounded. They had cornered Michael S_____ and they were beating him around the head with metal cap pistols. Michael was a bright kid with blonde hair and blue eyes. He was musically inclined and for the most part he minded his own business. I was friends with Michael and came to his rescue. I jumped in front of him and started swinging my fists at my classmates with the cap pistols. A smaller, younger kid was standing by, and, when I hit one of the kids who were attacking Michael and knocked him off balance, he fell on to the smaller kid's head and shoulder. This caused the younger kid's head to hit the surface of the brownstone tunnel. Blood squirted everywhere. Everyone ran, including me, yelling, "Look what you did." Darin was taken to a nearby home, and after his mother was called, he was taken to the hospital for stitches. I ran home and waited for the phone to ring. I told my grandfather what had happened and he told me not to worry, but he wished I hadn't run. The phone did ring! Darin's mom and my parents met and talked about what happened. I got hell for getting involved the way I did, and my grandfather praised me for rescuing Michael. It was the next morning that was the bummer. As I was about to go up stairs at the elementary school, to my fourth grade classroom, Ms. R_____ confronted me and began yelling at the top of her voice. She told all the first graders and everyone who could hear to stay away from me. I was walking trouble and a bully and didn't care about anyone but myself. I should be put in jail where I belong. Ms. R_____ had heard everything second and third hand. She asked no questions. I felt like it didn't matter what good I intended to do. I was just a bad boy, who would never be good enough! I sure was glad to leave that elementary school and go to a grade school way at the other end of the community.

The learning curve increased during those grade school years, particularly on the farm. At least there, I felt some sense of achievement. I could be helpful as another pair of hands, and I was appreciated. When I was around, I fed most of the animals, milked cows, helped to clean pens, and process milk. Between the ages of eight and nine, I learned to drive the small Ford tractor and began performing simple tasks that required the tractor (and needed to be done). These tests that I passed on the farm kept me progressing in the masculine mode, and I kept receiving positive and encouraging feedback. There were free periods of time that I could roam the woods and many times I would be on horseback. I loved this time more than any other on the farm. This time seemed to build up my resilience. I needed resilience to withstand the confrontations and the tests that I could expect at home and at school.

It wasn't at all clear what I was, certainly not to me, but I was no longer considered a sissy. I still got along with girls, even though I did not touch them, and I certainly did not play with them. There was a brief period of time, when I was home on an occasional weekend, that I would hangout at the community playground. The playground had the usual equipment in addition to a baseball field and a football field, and a full basketball court. A creek at the edge of the playground, polluted with waste from the glass factory, was an attracting feature. Kids always played in the creek, regardless of the pollution. We would try to dam up the water flow and build a step stone bridge across to the other side, which was private property. The weeds along the creek bank would grow fairly high by mid summer, and kids could lie down in the weeds and would not be seen. After I finished playing a game(s) for the afternoon, three girls, a twelve, thirteen, and fourteen year old, who lived on 14th Street near the playground, would approach me to lie down on the creek bank with them. They would unzip my pants and take turns fondling me, kissing and licking my penis. My genitals felt great being touched, and tickled, and licked. I, however, did not touch the girls, and I did not play with them. We hardly ever even talked to each other at any other time. Evidently, they decided that I was safe enough to experiment with. And yet, it was confusing to me because bad boys were always after girls for experimental, sexual encounters, but the reverse did not appear to be true to me. I did not approach them at any time. How did girls get away with sexual experimenting, but boys couldn't? Maybe the secret was that not all girls ran and told.

Even though these girls didn't tell, my past experience caused me to be doubtful. As an old friend used to ask, "Is the screwing you get worth the screwing you got?" I had paid dearly as a five year old, and four years later I could still remember the severe ostracization. No thank you!

In his book, *The Secret Life of Men*," Steve Biddulph, writes:

> Each morning, if the weather was fine, the man used to walk his six-year-old son to school. They lived in a quiet country town, and it was a beautiful downhill walk. The boy would skip and run about, pointing out birds, insect life, ripening blackberries. As they drew closer to the school, though, a curious change always came over the boy. A change that saddened the father, for he knew what it was. The boy's voice deepened, his shoulders tensed up, his face got serious. He was putting on the armor all males [in this culture] feel they must wear.[1]

A very real test that boys had to pass was proving that they were not going to be bullied around and that they had the right to be an individual and engage in activity independent of others. Steve Biddulph writes, "Imagine if being a woman meant having to fight . . . with any woman who came along?" This is, however, the test that boys in elementary through high school had to be prepared to pass. The irony of my elementary school kiss-off is that Darin's mother called my mother and asked if Darin invited me home after school, did I have her permission to come and stay for dinner? My mother told her that it was okay if I was not late coming home. I went with Darin to a well-known private estate where he and his mother were living. His dad wasn't around much and they lived in a huge house. I can tell you I was just a little nervous since I was being blamed for Darin's head injury. Darin and I had a brief period of goofing off before dinner. We were being observed at a yard game, although I was unaware and wouldn't have thought much about it even if I knew. It was after dinner, that Darin's mom began talking to me about Darin's situation. She owned and operated a rather large beauty salon in a nearby community. She, by necessity, had to work long hours and different schedules of hours, and Darin's father was often out of town, which meant she had to rely on her mother-in-law far too often to assist with Darin when he returned from school. Her proposal to me was that I come home with Darin and hangout with him until she or his father showed up. If it was dinnertime, I was to stay and have dinner and then go home. Darin's mother believed that since he was their only child, I could be like a big brother and teach him what it was like to be around other boys. "You need to smarten him up and toughen him up so he knows how to put on his boyhood armor." I would be paid $1.00 per hour. Back then, that was a lot of money for a nine and a half year old boy. She and my mom talked over the phone about it. My mom said it would be okay on a play-it-by-ear basis. It was a lot of responsibility for a boy. Darin's mom realized what had happened in the tunnel and that Darin kept trying to tell adults that I was not to blame, but none of the adults listened! Darin's mom believed that I was an intelligent and responsible boy and she trusted me, obviously.

The arrangement lasted for about six months, but activities and events that I wanted to do interfered, and with complete understanding my first employment situation ended. I was also informed by Darin's mom that she thought Ms. R_____ was a cruel person, who was sick in the head. After all the crap, it was nice to have a bit of affirmation!

Summer was coming and so was my tenth birthday. I would be moving on to a different school. Little did I know that I should be prepared for more non-academic tests to pass. The pecking order between boys would be starting all over again, when I got to a different school and a different mix of students. The changes to my internal map had to occur on a what's happening basis. I realized that I could not believe what I perceived one day and expect it to be the same tomorrow. I also realized that teachers gossip and pass on information about students from one grade to the next. It was decided that I was a lot like my brother, who had tried to choke one of his fifth grade teachers, and another one like him was on the way. I overheard the teachers talking on the first day of class and I had just arrived in the fifth grade. I knew they were talking about me, and when I asked a teacher if it was me they were talking about, she turned beet red and tried to mystify me.

Many of the tests of human development are, at least for men, a mix of skills that are academic, physical, and a measurement of masculinity. Once a male child enters into the first grade, a point of personal transformation (no matter how traumatic), he is placed on a learning curve. Only the increments of academic progress are formally reported with some pretense of objectivity. Otherwise, progress through incidental challenges of masculinity and physical capability are mostly subjective measurements that coerce American males to fit a pattern of cultural success and acceptance. Often, it is the incidental challenges (tests) of masculinity and physical capability that become more important than the development of the mind. Another warning about the confusion we are causing to the detriment of our American males, is our need to depend on public education systems to teach socialization skills. Our boys have little empathetic skills. There was a time when the socialization of a child amply occurred in the immediate and larger family. Do we need to reconsider what our priorities are when it comes to influencing the potential of males?

Chapter 6

The Conspiracy of the Fifties:
Challenging the Characteristics of Manhood

I think it is important for me to point out that until this place in the book, I've explained through my autobiography and relative research a perspective on what was and is expected of an All-American male. Another important aspect of my observations and perspective was what was considered an appropriate approach to relationships between my male peers and between men in general. I watched my older sister and her friends. I watched my mother and her sisters and female friends. They all hugged and kissed one another without fear or trepidation. At the same time, when I was in elementary school, I watched my older brother and his male friends. I watched my father and his father and my father's male friends. They shook hands, slapped each other on the back, and once in a great while, they would briefly give each other a stiff hug. I followed suit. Only women hugged me and kissed me, with one exception. My maternal grandfather hugged me and kissed me on the cheek. A long lasting impression was that men needed a purpose in order to be together. Men had to gather around an activity, which included any sport to playing cards or just watching the Super Bowl on TV. I have wondered if male companionship was only a spectator sport.

I was ten in 1950 and about to experience a whole redefinition of gender roles for adult males who were old enough to have served in WWII and were part of the American culture(s). Steve Biddulph, author of *The Secret Life of Men*, beginning his first chapter, "*The Problem,*" writes,

> MOST MEN DON'T have a life. Instead we have an act, an outer show, kept up for protection. We pretend things are fine, that everything is cool, and sometimes we even fool ourselves. But ask a man how he really feels or what he really thinks, and the first thing he thinks is "What am I supposed to say?" The average man today is deeply unhappy, but he would be the last to admit it.[1]

Biddulph goes on to suggest in his *Seven Steps to Manhood,* that one of the steps is: *Finding sacredness in your sexuality.*

> You have to find out how to be not just comfortable but transformed and fulfilled in your sexuality. Sex will either be a sleazy and obsessive part of your life or a sacred and powerful source of well-being. There isn't any in between. First you must relocate your sexual energy in yourself, instead of giving it away to women. Then you need to learn the art of the dance . . . . [2]

Does our pluralistic culture in America encourage the opportunity for men to be fulfilled in sexuality, to allow their sexuality to be a source of well-being, to really learn the art of the dance? Probably not! I know this, damn it, because I'm a man who grew up in this great country during the 1950s and was manipulated by cultural politics and gender roles being defined by others whom I never even met. Most of our ancestors escaped to America in search of freedom, and that freedom is being violated in the lives of our American men today in very dangerous ways. Am I expressing anarchist philosophy or being over-reactive to the erosion of our constitutional rights? I don't think so! Just watch the amount of TV commercials that portray men as the typical buffoons of modern life. Beyond these mockeries of American males, the ultimate insult is the commercial where a woman is advertising *Levitra* for sexually dysfunctional males. What do women know about it really? They never had to "get it up"! Maybe some women can minimally imagine what it feels like for a male on the inside, but that's it!

I want to share some of the witnesses to what I'm writing about with you from LIFE Magazine, the proof in pictures. In the magazine article, "Masculinity Under Fire," written by John Ibson in the 2001 edition of *Life's Looking at Life*, examines *Life's Presentation of Camaraderie and Homoeroticism Before, During, and After the Second World War*. The article begins by summarizing Allen Drury's best selling novel, *ADVISE and CONSENT*. In the novel, Senator Brigham Anderson explains to his wife that during the war he had a love affair with another man. Although his wife refers to the love affair as a "horrible thing," the senator did not at all agree with the description of his wife. He, nevertheless, commits suicide. He could not endure the pressure of his [American] culture after WWII.[3]

"Although WWII subverted traditional gender prescriptions . . . regarding American male relationships with one another, once the war ended though, attachments allowed or even promoted in wartime were discouraged or rendered sinister."[4]

"On an unprecedented scale, the war seriously challenged America's tidy dichotomizing of erotic expression into heterosexual and homosexual realms."[5]

Men, who were deeply intimate with another man, especially if that intimacy were romantic, had become culturally sinister, and it had not been as sinister in the nineteenth century. Increasingly, pressures on men to inhibit intimacy with each other had grown intense. Men too cozy with each other were suspiciously like women. They were sissies, probably homosexuals, words that had not even existed for the most part in the Victorian Era.

An historical example of male relationships in the Victorian Era is depicted by Admiral Mahan and Samuel Ashe of the US Navy. They maintained a romantic relationship of forty years before the Civil War. Mahan and Ashe had been involved at a time when a relationship like theirs had different consequences and connotations than such a romance between men would acquire later on.

"[Evidently,] situational homosexuality—as is all of sexuality or even human expression itself, [is] a matter of place and time."[6]

A psychologist and veteran, Irving L. Janis, observed that a man entering the army undergoes as profound a change in his way of life as he is likely to experience in his entire adult lifetime. Beth Bailey and David Farber, historians, have written that the gulf between men and women was specifically created by WW II. "The war brought the differences between men's and women's lives into sharp contrast . . . . men fought. Women didn't."[7]

> The war and/or the wartime period gave a peculiar intensity to men's relationships. There was an observable tenderness between men that was no doubt as common in war as it was rare in civilian life . . . . The many "thousand pictures" of men together that appeared during WW II, as well as those representations of men that appeared immediately before and after it, constitute a largely overlooked and often denied chapter in the history of twentieth century American sexuality. Most importantly, perhaps, the photographs form a chapter in the little-understood history of men's relationships with each other, unions that may have been erotic more often than realized though less often than feared.[8]

In Douglas Allenbrook's memoir, *"See Naples,"* he calls testimony to profound friendships formed during or in anticipation of battle. He writes of men who had "what some of us called, without malice, a second marriage." Allenbrook reminds us without saying so that it is just as inhibiting to believe that intimacy must involve sex as it is to insist that it dare not. It is an implicit point in some of Life's [magazine] wartime pictures.[9]

One of the significant points in Allenbrook's memoir is his recollection of his friendship with Leonard, who died shortly after arriving at Naples. Leonard had apparently beckoned to Allenbrook to join him as they slept outdoors on a December night in Italy. Allenbrook recalls, "He was cold; he wanted me. Together we would be warm." Regretfully, he failed to accept this particular offer of intimacy, and it seems to be a patterned inhibition, an essential pattern that controls his emotion for the rest of his life.[10]

> In the movies of the 1950's the replacement of the Bob Hope—Bing Crosby duo was Dean Martin and Jerry Lewis. They starred together in the 1953 film, *The Caddy.* They seldom interacted intimately and their friendship rendered them ridiculous. Nevertheless, genuine affection is suggested when together they sing, "What Would You Do Without me?" Lines in the song include, "We will be just like lovers, you and I." However, this was the fifties and not the forties; and the song had to end with the men pummeling each other to the point of demolishing their straw hats.[11]

There were scenes between men in American films of the 1940s that were more compelling and intimate than those played for laughs by Kelly and Sinatra, and Andrew and Kaye. In the film, *Red River*, there was the symbolic marriage between John Wayne and Montgomery Clift as ranch partners. The most significant ending phrase is, "You two know you love each other." Though it was unlikely, in film, women seemed to be the target of the dynamics of thwarted male affection in post-war America. Surely at no time before the Second World War had so many American men consciously felt deep affection for other males, and not since the previous century had romantic attachments between men been so wide-spread and received such little scorn. Further, perhaps at no time since the war has affection between men been as culturally unencumbered as it was from 1941 to 1945.[12]

> These affectionate relationships between men were threatening during peacetime, challenging as they did the cultural imperative that had had enormous power since the late nineteenth century. Authentic men were to be strong, and above all else, they had to be doing manly work that was to be the antithesis of womanly endeavor. The cult of toughness and the particular cultural reinforcements associated with it eventually gave open affection between men a bad name, quite literally—and only in America. Weakness and loving other men is not necessarily an inevitable equation, but more of an assumption. And yet, it was, of course, the one that took root in nineteenth century America . . . . [13]

Bothersome males like me, who seemed to push or stretch the culturally enforced boundaries, did not fit into the rigidly defined dichotomies about sexuality. Yes, I was one who would express his love for friends whether male or female in a rather open manner. But I otherwise met the job requirements for maleness and did not appear to be stereotypically homosexual, which I wasn't. Generally speaking, I had homosexual experiences in my lifetime. Did I choose that cultural way of life? Obviously not! And, I am not at all sure that homosexuality is a matter of choice. We do not know if homosexuality is the result of biological or psycho/sociological factors or both. The essential issue in the post war years and in the 1950s, then, was not sexuality as such, but gender roles and their post war reconstruction concepts. Our pluralistic culture(s) were freshly demonizing same sex affection, and these demons or bugaboos were charged with keeping everyone in compliance with convention or else—suffer.

John Horne Burns, author of *The Gallery*, had his novel focus on the world of soldiers who openly loved each other. He also wrote *Lucifer with a Book* and *A Cry of Children*. It was *Lucifer with a Book* that proved to be his downfall, because it drew venomous criticism. Later, it was Gore Vidal, who was no fan of Burns, that wrote, "*Lucifer with a Book* was perhaps the most savagely and unjustly attacked book of its day." The attackers were part of the postwar mood in America engaging in literary criticism that flatly refused to tolerate all eroticized love between men.[14] When I read this report, I had to ask myself, "Did these critics ever read in the Old Testament, King David's lament over the death of Jonathan?" Were they involved in an intimate relationship? (Read First Samuel in the Bible)

What is interesting about the decade of the 1950s in America, a decade very similar to the years, 2001-2004, is that the decade's three principal symbols of overripe Americanism and its moralism, Senator Joseph McCarthy, Francis Cardinal Spellman, and J. Edgar Hoover, have themselves all been the subject of considerable speculation and innuendo about unconventional sexuality.

By the time the 50's were over, I was twenty years old and a junior in college. But I watched how long it took for America to begin to respond sanely to these ruthless men, who played fast and loose with our constitutional rights and our personal freedoms. Ought not men's expressions be given the same grace period, at least? Perhaps, our conservative groups wouldn't need to create power plays against the majority of men in this country, if they realized that the majority of men contribute an enormous amount of energy, creativity, and personal sacrifice to make this wonderful experiment called the United States work.

John Ibson, author of Life's article, "*Masculinity Under Fire,*" concludes his expose' by writing that,

> Life's [pictorial] wartime rendering of masculinity existed, like wartime maleness itself, as a thing apart—more tender, more cooperative, more frolicsome, and much more affectionate. The pity was [and is] that this hiatus from the cold confinements of modern masculinity could not continue in times of peace.[14]

Matthew McKay, Ph.D., is a director of Haight Ashbury Psychological Services and Brief Therapy Associates in San Francisco, and Patrick Fanning, who is a professional writer in the mental health field and the founder of a men's support group in northern California, make this comment in their book, *Being a Man,*

Male friendships are difficult to form and maintain, especially after age thirty. Many reasons have been advanced to explain this difficulty. Some say that men are too competitive, that they would rather dominate than relate. Others say that heterosexual men are too homophobic to risk making friendly overtures to other men, lest their expressions of interest be interpreted as seductive. Some point out that man's thirties and forties are the age of accomplishment and nest building, a time to focus on career and family to the exclusion of friendship. Still others point out that our culture actually ridicules and discourages male friendships. For example, TV shows and movies repeatedly depict the man who maintains friendships outside his home as immature, selfish guy who deserts his wife and children to hang out with his juvenile, low-class pals.

Perhaps male friendships languish because few people, male or female, really value it. Think of all the jokes about "male bonding" that imply it is a somewhat crude, primitive, silly, and perhaps dangerous thing to do. Think about the stereotypes of men who can't relate except when drinking beer, discussing sports, or playing poker. It's too bad. Because you need male friends. A close male friend offers a special kind of comfortable intimacy that cannot be supplied by a woman. Only another man can understand exactly what you mean when you talk about your sexual desires, your mixed feelings toward your children, your fears about your job, your disappointment in failure, your secrets you can share with a male friend that you can't share with your wife or girlfriend or mother. Having meaningful relationships with other men validates your worth as a man. It raises your self-esteem and lets you know that you are not alone.[15]

At the beginning of the 50s, when I was ten, my best friend died. My maternal grandfather expired, and I felt entirely alone and abandoned at home. Women in my family tried to comfort and console me, but from my father and uncles, there was nothing unless silence counts for something. Even more time was spent on the farm.

Chapter 7

Beyond Acceptance:

The Unacceptable and the Act of Accepting

Acceptance is one of the most important key issues in the process of *Growing Up Male In America*. In the last chapter, I tried to open up the controversy about how men were expected to evolve into their roles of masculinity and at the same time distance themselves from any romantic/eroticized male-to-male relationships. The manipulation of male development by the religious patriotic cultures and the politicized evangelistic cultures has little or no empathy for the male situation of this nation. Having been manipulated since WW II, the bothersome males like me may need to know the verification of our history (what's for real?). The observation of our historical manipulation in pictures and in the expression of the fine arts, literature, theater, and film cannot be denied.

After the death of my maternal grandfather, the remaining time in the fifth grade was a complete loss. My academic performance was non-existent. However, by the following September when I found myself in the sixth grade, much to my surprise, my teachers told me that I was promoted because they believed in me. I did not disappoint them. As a male, I remember this consideration as a major, positive break for me in the most unexpected place.

In junior high school, I began to feel better and better about myself and, perhaps, even discovered a modicum of ego that escaped the constant scoldings for being overbearing, bull-headed, and a big-mouth. I found out that part of being a masculine twelve year old was doing well academically, while at the same time being disruptive in certain classes. I sensed that I was being accepted or approved of by my peers.

Although I didn't know it then, my early childhood manipulation was already at work in junior high school. On Saturday nights a whole gang of my friends would go over to another section of town to the roller skating rink. That's where I met her. She attended the same junior high. When it was an all couples skate, she got a girlfriend to suggest that I ask her to skate with me. That was my first, although brief, encounter with puppy love. My hormones were roaring and so were hers. But, alas, I was rather timid. What I mean to say is that the sound of voices screaming in my head from my early childhood, "You're bad, no playing with girls, don't you dare touch them," continued to echo in my memory. No one told me that petting or heavy petting was now acceptable. My first attempt at being a steady Romeo probably lasted four months. She was patient with me, but I wasn't offering much of what she was sure I could give her. Five years later, we got together and made-up for the lost opportunities. The confusion over what is acceptable behavior for young men, however, still continues without regard for the fallout and its damaging effects on the development of American males. No, instead the moralistic manipulators nationally and locally use their moralism and religiosity to polarize male behavior on a continuum of homosexuality to heterosexuality. If a guy is identified as a homosexual, then he simultaneously is unfortunately weak, sick, and evil. And, if a guy is heterosexual, he is a candidate for success if he is appropriately aggressive, if he is strong, competitive and has a handsome physique. Who says this polarization is valid? The American Psychological Association no longer says so. The American Psychotherapist Association, of which I am a member, does not say so. The five other national mental health related associations, of which I am a member, do not say so. A relatively few reputable professionals in the mental health field and a large number of fundamental, conservative Christian evangelists, perhaps because of their own sexual insecurity, say so!

There are eleven slightly different, primary definitions of the term/word *accept*. The verb form *accept* explains the intentional behavior of a person or group of persons more than the noun form *acceptance*. The on-line computer dictionary, Miriam Webster (2004), lists many applications of the term/word *accept*. I would like to share a few of these applications with you, because they represent the context and meaning of the way I will be using *accept* as an action concept.

> *To accept means to:*
> "Consent or assent to a condition,
> Admit into a group or community,
> Approval despite complete satisfaction,
> Allow participation in or the right to be part of,
> Tolerate or accommodate oneself to,
> Show respect towards."
> (Unabridged Dictionary)

Any one of the above meanings can be applied to the manner in which the term/word *accept* will be used in this chapter and throughout the book. These meanings will be implied when the noun form of the word—*acceptance* is used as well.

Since I don't believe that a person is purely any one thing, I will rarely use labels for descriptions except when it is expedient to do it in our American culture(s). It matters not to me if you are a sissy, fag, queer, closet queen, gay, homosexual, bisexual, bicurious, an all-American red-blooded male, a champion of some sort, a red neck, an average guy, or whatever label is laid upon you, because you are different. We all pay lip service to phrases like, "No one is perfect, don't judge others lest you be judged, the American Constitution protects an individual's rights, persons deserve a certain amount of respect, etc." But this is not what we do, is it? Freedom and liberty for the American male is defined by how well he conforms to the masculine expectations of others or he knows the evaluation and judgment will be harsh. During some research I was doing in the library on masculinity, I came across several books that attempted to propose theory and method for preventing homosexuality. I was immediately challenged to read these theories and methods.

Sooner or later it is explained to the reader that the premise for writing is the resulting dissatisfaction men have with their homosexual lifestyle. The manner of the interviews conducted and what male population was included or excluded was not reported. This was the basis for their investigative authority. It was the consensus of these investigators, who were reportedly credentialed in some field of psychological study, that the conditions for a man to be produced as a homosexual were existent in his childhood and therefore laid the foundation for his homosexual feelings and/or tendencies.

The wry titles of these books suggest and presume that homosexual behavior is a viral disease to be prevented and our (male) children need to be inoculated against it.

The authors go on to indicate that the gay life style did not work for those men and that they all suspected that there were conditions in their childhood that laid the foundation for their homosexual feelings. Okay, I said to myself, I have been doing professional counseling/therapy since 1965 until the present and I'm saying something different. I have counseled a large number of gay men in my 39 years of counseling/therapy and many of these men were in different places along the continuum of polarization. I recognize that there are life positions of dissatisfaction, since gay men are not accepted in supposedly straight cultures of America. Gay men obviously experience rejection. There are men who leave the heterosexual culture having had children, and now gay, are quite possibly limited in their contact with their children. There are gay men, who want very much to participate in the rearing of children, but must sacrifice this opportunity because of their life-style. Probably, my family would not accept me if I participated in the gay life style, and the community I grew up in would not be supportive. If I were gay, how in the hell could I expect to be contentedly satisfied? I have listened to slightly more heterosexual men in counseling, who are struggling with their married, cohabitant, relationships and who are equally dissatisfied. The issue of masculinity does not primarily involve sexual orientation. The issue of masculinity is a larger issue than cultural manipulation and expectation.

Too much of what has been written indicates to me that there is a *blame game* being played and the American male, American family, and especially the American homosexual are all the scapegoats. The authors go on to imply that it is not healthy to encourage our children "To be all that they can be." Rather, this concept of freedom and liberty is construed by the authors into a means of perpetuating outdated gender stereotyping.

I am sure we can agree that the human race, although designed male and female, is more complicated that discarding those who are gay as a third gender. These authors who over-simplify the conditions for preventing developing homosexual behavior can do so only because their view of a sanctimonious family unit is simple and non-existent.

One of the significant ingredients of prevention is to preserve the family unit ideal—mother father, and a reasonable number of children (perhaps no more than four). I do not believe the population of American has ever produced very many perfect families. We have far more dysfunctional family units. More typically, family units contained at least a grandparent or aunt or uncle or an extended family member. Placing elderly parents and family members in nursing homes and facilities of extended care is more of a recent phenomenon (70's to present).

However, looking at history with a different perspective can result in a more broadened view. In what way does evolutionary processes dictate the sexual behaviors of a man or a woman except for procreation? Men and women both have demonstrated that their sex drive is not just a matter of animal instinct. They have many and varied opportunities and options and do exercise their choices.

I'm sorry, but I don't agree that we can just dismiss the faults of the American family in order to extol its virtuous nurturance. No, not when in recent years we have had to change the laws in order to protect children from all kinds of parental abuses. Many of the American males did not have the good fortune of having adult men around in their developmental growth period. On the other hand, it might have been a good thing if the absence of fathers meant relief from abuse.

I've read ancient history as well as modern history, and I don't understand how we can over look the various forms and practice of homosexual behavior in the Greek and Roman empires. It was an acceptable practice for a male whether married or not to couple with another male. A married man could and often would have a manservant, which more often than not included an eroticized relationship. Apparently, heterosexual men inter-mingled with homosexual men without being threatened and feeling insecure. Many women, even in our society, find it easier to embrace various male relationships among men than do the American males. I do not believe that choosing a particular sexual orientation is simply a matter of decision for any American male. Homosexuality in any shape or form is simply not a matter of choice. People tend to do what it is that they want to do or are prone to do. Dr. Victor Frankl, holocaust survivor, physician, and author of *Logotherapy* and *Man's Search for Meaning* has sufficiently demonstrated that people while threatened and manipulated will comply; however, as soon as the threat is removed individuals will do what it is they want to do.

What is being accomplished by the manipulation of American males? We are not born *tabula rasa*, a blank tablet upon which life writes our destiny. We are born with a pool of genes with certain potentials and propensities, which most likely will be influenced by our dysfunctional family life and our dysfunctional, pluralistic, American culture. I don't believe, as I once did, that it is my obligation to fit in and comply in order to avoid hate crimes, harassment, discrimination, and shunning by cultures in the United States that only pay lip service to the values of freedom and liberty represented in the US constitution, while treating different American males unequally. I am an American male, and whatever else I am, I am supposedly to be treated with respect regardless of my differences. And, my differences are to be tolerated because I am a human being who has human rights that are not to be violated. On the planet earth, America is the foremost advocate of human rights. Are we hypocritical? As an American male, I am a combination of many different talents, capacities, environmental influences, choices, and desires. I am a complex individual who may not fit into specific patterns and may change in any given period of time in an unpredictable, immeasurable, and unrepeatable way, but will I be acceptable? As a bothersome American male who does not fit the pattern of typical developmental growth, just give me a label and quite likely I will not be acceptable. Perhaps because of writing this book that advocates freedom, liberty, and equality for all American males, I will not be accepted by some. So be it!

What is unacceptable? To me the most heinous, personal, sexual behavior that sick American males are known to engage in is pedophile activity and rape. Of course, crimes like murder, manslaughter and robbery are obviously unacceptable to all culture groups in America. Nevertheless, when it comes to sexual offenses, the various cultures of America are unpredictable on most any continuum. Recently, while advocating for the admission of homosexuals to positions of ordination in the Presbyterian Church USA, I was asked these questions in an open forum:

> Dr. Patton, do you have children?" "Yes," I said, "My wife and I have two adult children—a daughter and a son." "Suppose when they were 6 or 7 years old, you were notified that a male Sunday school teacher of your congregation molested one of your children. What would you think or how would you feel?"
>
> "At first, I would be devastated and then I would turn my energy to complete empathy for my child, and then I would feel rage and would need to control it. I would insist on some program of rehabilitation."
>
> Now, I said, "Let me ask you a few questions. How did we get from homosexuality to pedophilia? What did you assume about homosexuality? What myths do you believe as truth about either pedophilia or homosexuality?" Perhaps, phobias have a greater influence on us than we realize.

Just for the record, I want to share some rather generally known information about pedophilia. Although pedophilia occurs more frequently with men, it ought not to be assumed that women are not involved too. Pedophilia is a reoccurring sexual arousal and desires or fantasies that involve sexual impulses toward a pre-adolescent child or children. The pedophile must be above age sixteen, and the sexual attraction must involve a child of age thirteen and younger. The molested child must be at least five years younger than the person considered to be an adult. A pedophile is sexually aroused because the child is a child, regardless of the pedophile's sexual orientation, or the child's gender. Although pedophiles engage in or fantasize about same-sex children, they very rarely participate in heterosexual adult sexual relations, and they deny being homosexual. If you wish to have even more information, you can refer to The Human Sexuality WEB on the Internet.

It is unacceptable to me that when discussing sexual orientation, the discussion turns immediately to body parts rather than to life experiences, contributions, social stability, and basic human rights of equality that are to be upheld by the Constitution of the United States. Right now, religious cultures/denominations and even the Congress of the U.S. is debating the issue of same sex marriage. President Bush says, "Our nation must defend the sanctity of marriage." The honorable Congressman from Tucson, Arizona, Jim Kolbe, Republican; however, says,

> Let's be clear about one thing: An amendment to the U.S. Constitution to restrict marriages is not about protecting the 'sanctity' of the institution of marriage. No marriage between a man and a woman will be jeopardized by giving legal standing to a similar commitment by two persons of the same gender.[3]
>
> It is unacceptable to me when a significant number of well-meaning people in this country allow their religious belief to be politicized into a subversive tool by narcissistic, political leaders. Patriotic religiosity has far more possibility of harming the historical experiment that is the republic of the United States than any American male sexual orientation.

It is not acceptable to me to even imagine that so many men are unaware of their actual situation in America:

- Though few men are aware of it, men's life expectancy has dropped dramatically as compared with women's over the last several decades, . . .

- Annual statistics show that America's leading fatal diseases target men far more often than women, . . .
- Men are the primary victims of crime, violence, and murder, . . .
- Men comprise the vast majority of those killed or seriously injured on the job, . . .
- America's men are far more likely than its women to suffer from alcohol or drug addiction, . . .
- Recent studies show that men are chronically under diagnosed for depression and other mental diseases, . . .
- Males in the United States are the suicide sex, . . .
- The health and violence crisis for African-American men is especially acute,
- Boys in the United States are diagnosed and treated for a variety of behavioral and mental disorders far more frequently than girls, . . .
- America's young men (ages fifteen to twenty-four) are far more likely than women of the same age group to commit suicide or become addicted to alcohol and drugs, . . .
- Hundreds of thousands of young men are taking steroids and growth hormones, . . .
- Men are suffering an epidemic of sexual dysfunction, . . .
- Despite the view that boys are favored in the classroom, boys are faring far worse than girls in our nation's schools, . . .
  Men are now less likely than women to attend college and less likely to graduate from college, . . .
- This generation has witnessed a dramatic drop in real wages for the average working man, while that of women have increased, . . .
- Recent economic trends have left millions of men permanently unemployed or underemployed,
- Male heads of households now have less net worth than women who head households, . . .
- The economic and social crisis for men is especially dire for African-American men, . . .
- The millions of American male veterans who have returned home from the war with broken bodies or minds have been grossly neglected, . . .
- The problem of homelessness is primarily a problem of single adult men, . . .
- Millions of fathers have lost meaningful contact with their children as family courts discriminate against men in child custody decisions, . . .

- Men are increasingly torn between the necessities of their job and their desire to have time for their families, . . . Men face serious discrimination in the criminal justice system, . . .
- The increasing number of men now heading single-parent households are given virtually no social or government support, . . .
- As life in the workplace "harness" undermines men's health and their ability to parent, it also makes men obsolete after they retire."[4]

I will ask again, what is being accomplished and who is benefiting by trying to inhibit and restrict the American male, regardless of his sexual orientation, into a prescribed gender role profile? Is what has been described above an acceptable picture of desirable masculinity? Although subtle, has this chapter described a form of rape of the American male, a true crisis? More harassment, more suspicion, more restriction, more straight-jacket tactics will do more harm than healing. It will take a great deal more understanding and empathy, after there is acceptance, before healing will really take place. I am an American male, who is a citizen of the United States of America. Am I acceptable to you despite my differences? In your heart and in your conscience if you accept me and you tolerate me, will I enjoy the same privileges that you do?

Chapter 8

The Castrated Pleaser

And the Good Ol' Boys' Club

W ho benefits from keeping the American male in cultural straightjackets? Someone does benefit or this massive effort would not have occurred and would not be still occurring. And, what is it that is individually or collectively gained or received as a benefit? There probably are several significant groups in America that are in a position to benefit.

Women are one of the most significant beneficiaries. It is not long before the male infant understands that he will get what he wants when and if he is cooperative in giving his mother what she wants. This process of the learning curve necessarily has to continue in order to assimilate the child into society. What else happens though? The male child learns how to interpret the world around him through his mother's eyes and through her emotional responses. We now have an imprinting. That is, the male child has participated in a "Perceptual Learning" experience. This imprinting, and the perception and interpretation of it, may be reversible, however, it is unlikely or difficult to change at best.

Is there sufficient information to know what imprinting processes will serve the American male well later on in his life? For example, what if the aggressive behavior in male toddlers is controlled and redirected to the point that they become less than assertive. The object of their emotions becomes blurred and bent. I do therapy with men who far too often do not know what to feel when they have been imposed upon. I know young men in their late twenties and thirties who are still deferring their own, personal decisions to their parents or their wives and/or cohabitants. They are dependently related and/or co-dependently related. These are American males who are starved for approval from their fathers, who are slow to realize this need for support because they never received it from their fathers, who will not break the cross-generational pattern. These are co-dependent American males who learn to comfort themselves by excessiveness, addiction to food, addiction to promiscuity, addiction to illegal substances and alcohol. In a utopian land of promises, many of us have been sold the idea, to some degree, that we ought to be compensated in some way because we deserve it. Yes, I believe that women, mothers in particular, benefit from the castrating straightjackets they help construct for the American males to wear.

According to Gary Taylor, author of *Castration*, American women envy other American women who have a eunuch for a husband. His interpretation of a vasectomy, which he has received, is the act of becoming neutered. Historically, *castration* is not necessarily the total removal of the testicles, but rather it is the removal of the ability to impregnate. A eunuch husband has a functional penis but dysfunctional testicles.[1]

Taylor opens the discussion "of what is the meaning of the word man," by writing

> Whatever its form, self-castration remains, for the male majority, simply incomprehensible. As the rhetoric of "real men" demonstrates, the uncastrated do not even know what to call a castrated human being. He resists definition. Is he still male? Is [he] it still human? . . . That bewilderment did not originate in the 1990's; it has a long loud, angry history . . . Real men have been raging against unreal men for millennia . . . How can a man know how he should *act* without knowing what he should *be*? And how can anyone "be a man" without knowing what the word *man* means?[2]

I would like to add my own theoretical proposition and/or educated guess to the American male's current situation, which causes some of his confusion as to how he becomes neutered in ways other than the surgeon's scalpel.

After listening to the testimony of many young men whom I have counseled and some of whom I had the privilege of mentoring, I found that an abusive or absent or neglectful father or any combination of the above was a significant aspect of these young men's codependency. Their sense of self-worth and sense of self-esteem were at all-time lows because they wanted and needed approval from their fathers which they kept trying to get, only to be repeatedly disappointed. After a while, the goal of their aspirations dissolved into codependent behavior. They discovered that there were other ways of getting approval. They could gather around themselves a group of drinking buddies. The alcohol provided a means of escape from the haunting lack of approval from significant male images in their lives. Drinking was often combined with other available substances to intensify the "chill out" effect. The need for approval would be temporarily numbed, and there was comfort in the fact that their buddies were similar to them. Those who benefited from the creation and support of these addicted American male subcultures were and are the friendly, neighborhood bartenders who were serving these young men out the back door when they were under-aged teenagers. Drug traffickers, many of whom are members of the *Good Ol' Boys' Club*, find sales to young men very profitable. We all know some of the beneficiaries; they are judges, police officers, lucrative business owners, corporate executives, and attorneys, who may be members of the country club poker club, to mention a few. Their motivation is greed, the accumulation of wealth.

And yet, the need for approval continued beyond the meager encouragement and identity that was gathered from their peers. Where else could they look for a sense of approval? Aha! They could leap from one bed to another. They could get to be good lovers with enough practice, and they would be approved of by women. After all, their mothers approved of them for the most part. But, at last, even being good at promiscuity and risking disease did not fill the void of approval from significant males in their lives. The codependency continues and will continue until the American males learn that there are other options and possibilities. Usually, after intervening therapy, men begin to understand that they do not necessarily need approval from their father (guardian/parent image). For these men, it is probably a waste of time to seek approval from fathers, because most often sons will not get their father's approval anyway. There are viable substitutes, like an uncle, a teacher, a coach, a college professor, or any other mentor.

Of course, there is another way to get approval. They could become pleasers. They could find some unsuspecting persons to whom they could eventually turn over the management of their lives. By being kind, generous, and pleasing to others, they will be seduced into dependency and never realize the price of personal freedom that they pay as they give approval.

Figuratively speaking, there are many choices for approval seeking. American males may even resort to castrating themselves. Ass kissing, promiscuity, and addictions are just a few ways of seeking approval. Taylor says,

> Most men's experiences do not fit the definition of *man* we have inherited. Is that because something has gone wrong with the world or because something was always wrong with the world? Every man's self-assurance, his sense of ethical and practical direction, depends upon a definition, a point of orientation outside himself—whether he identifies that personal North Pole as the tradition of a people or the biology of a species or the commandment of a god. Consequently, whenever we lose our way we retrace our steps until we can realign ourselves in relation to that magnetic point of orientation.[3]

As mentioned earlier, we are asked to realize that how a male perceives the external messages of his environment and interprets them internally is a critical translation of what it means to be a man. Throughout history and culture confusion has occurred. For example, in the gospel of Matthew in the nineteenth chapter at verse twelve, Jesus speaks of eunuchs or castration, and Saint Augustine, one of the most significant theologians of all Christian history, asks how to name, define, or explain this kind of human being. Does this pondering over neutered males (eunuchs) suggest that they were less than men? At the very end of the nineteenth century, Nietzsche explains that the Church has attacked the [very] passions [of men], [and] to attack the passions at their [very] roots means to attack life at its roots: "*The practice of the Church is hostile to life.*"[4] Perhaps the Church is also a beneficiary of harnessing men, which enables the clergy in power to press males into molds that will serve the mission of the Church, as corrupt as the Church may be from time to time.

While I agree with Taylor, who says in so many words that males are reassured by a definition, a point of orientation outside themselves, I believe that this behavioral/observable evidence is what is a confusing and self-defeating factor for most American males. The translation of the external messages to the internal sense of reality can no longer be trusted. I firmly believe that a sense of direction and a sense of identity and values ought to be influenced by the external environment. The choice of direction, the choice of what is most valued/cherished, the choice of what is most meaningful, having been appropriately informed, needs to be internal and then translated to the external environment in which one lives. When the external environment becomes the primary orientation of one's sense of being, the seduction of castration begins, at least figuratively.

When I was a kid, a teenager, a college student, and perhaps until I was a graduate student, I was overly impressed and respectful of individuals with positions of authority, with positions of knowledge, and with positions of accomplishment. Titles demanded an engrained and profuse acknowledgement of some sort from me. How a change in me occurred, I am not quite sure. It was probably because I was becoming one of those persons I had esteemed so highly. However, the change enabled me to see more realistically the humanity of those I admired and esteemed beyond what was reasonably deserved. It is no surprise to me that I had been allowing myself to be defined by some focal point outside of me, which was in no way as informed internally about me as I was.

I must relate a personal story when I was being forced into some career identity by a number of supposedly highly regarded instruments. The only controlled circumstances of the tests, as nearly as I could tell, were that the test instruments were to be timed and each individual student was invited into the junior high school counselor's office, no matter what the time of day or the interruption of the student's schedule. At the time I was asked to participate in the tests, I was feeling quite ill. I was informed that this was the scheduled time for my tests, which were mandatory. What did I want others to think of me? Did I want the guidance counselor and others to think of me as some kind of pansy? Of course, with that kind of possible judgment, I went on with the tests. The next day I was diagnosed with pneumonia. When I returned to school and was asked to go to the guidance counselor's office for the results, I was told that I failed the tests miserably and that I would be lucky to be hired as a truck driver, if I could get a driver's license. At the time, I thought he was deliberately putting truck drivers down and not just me. In the process of scheduling my courses for the following year in the college prep curriculum, my father had to call the school and tell my guidance counselor to "stick the test results up his ass." My father insisted on my college prep courses, and I was enrolled with no questions asked. The guidance counselor told me that I would not succeed because it would be like being hit in the face with a baseball bat and I couldn't take it. Years afterwards, I would send him newspaper write-ups about by academic and career accomplishments. I quit this gloating when I figured he was dead. I found out over a period of time that he and my father had never been friends. I cannot even imagine where I would be today if my father or I had allowed that person and his mind set to define who I was going to be. This is what I mean when I object to one's point of orientation for his life's journey and meaning to lie outside himself. I could have, figuratively speaking, been castrated. The reason why we need to be informed about being disenfranchised is to discover what it means to be an assertive and courageous male.

Gary Taylor, in further discussion of castration/vasectomy holds the writings of Thomas Middleton's works as highly creditable documentation of how the "Renaissance," the "Reformation," the "scientific revolution," and the "modern" were fused together in the play, *A Game at Chess.* In summary, the play symbolically dramatizes the Reformation as a struggle between black and white chess pieces. Taylor says,

> In a single text, *A Game of Chess,* brings together most of the elements—in religion, literature, art, philosophy, politics, economics—that transformed medieval Christendom into the modern world order . . . Its treatment of male sexuality also epitomizes an era. In the thirteenth and fourteenth centuries, the Church had mobilized all its resources against the Cathar heresy, which regarded the human body—and the genitals especially—as a creation of Satan, not God; Cathar denied the corporeality of Jesus. In reaction the Church began systematically stressing and celebrating the incarnation of a Christ fully enfleshed, from toenails to testicles. Painting and sculpture from the fourteenth to the sixteenth centuries pay extraordinary tribute (documented by art historian Leo Steinberg) to the genitals of Jesus. Michelangelo's *Risen Christ*, for instance, stands completely, full-frontally, unashamedly nude. But with the Counter-Reformation shame triumphed; by order of Pope Paul IV, "many beautiful and antique statues" in Rome were—as Montaigne reports—"castrated."[5]

Perhaps, none of this would matter except that this history shapes, in its existential reality, attitudes about what it means to be a man. What it means to be a man, just as what it means to be castrated, has not always stayed the same. The two most influential theorists of sexuality in the twentieth century, Freud and Foucault, cannot answer what it means to be a man and/or a castrated man. What we know is that the power to impregnate is the power to create evolutionary change. Apparently, Freud thought of castration as a genital loss that all women believe they have suffered and all men fear to suffer.[6]

Believe it or not, the Reformation was fought, in part, over sex—over male sexuality. Luther, Calvin, Henry III, and the other Protestant leaders were all men. They refused to become allegorical eunuchs. The supremacy of celibacy advocated by the Roman Catholic Church was denied. Instead, these men demanded the right to marry the women they wanted.

As the search continues for the definition of what a man is, it ought to be noted that in humanist Europe, as in previous societies, it was the scrotum that was attacked and/or mutilated in order to redefine or determine manhood/masculinity. However, in the twentieth-century psychoanalysis, castration was reinterpreted as an attack on the penis. Although there is some verbal hangover in phrases that are often used like, "You really got balls!" or "Have you got enough balls?" There is much more focus in our society on the size of the penis. Hence, advertisements for penis enlargement remark, "Size really does matter." Or intimidating, slang remarks among males might be phrased, "So you think your dick is big enough?" This consciousness about the size of our genital body parts certainly influences our idea(s) of what it means to be a man. Nevertheless, there were some cultural changes and some medical technologies that diminished the power of the scrotum. Most of these changes had to do with reproduction. The advent of improved condoms, the pill, and other various methods of birth control, as well as artificial insemination and sperm banks, greatly reduced the important status of the scrotum.

While the scrotum is the "family jewel chamber" which determines the male fertility, by contrast it is the penis that gives pleasure to the male. Does what it means to be a man include his ability to enjoy a fertile orgasm of remarkable pleasure? Male preoccupation with pornography seems to indicate the potential of this possibility. In closing, Taylor offers this anecdotal question to his research into the castration of western manhood, "What does manhood mean in the twenty-first century?" I, personally, think that the question cannot be answered completely. We know attitudinally, at least, it means do not be an ass-kisser (if at all possible) and it means not to rely on an egotistical pride regarding your anatomical physique and an exaggerated view of your genitals. Being a man does not include being codependent and allowing yourself to be addictively defined by someone else's orientation, sense of direction, and commitment. And then Taylor responds to the question, "What does manhood mean in the twenty-first century?" by saying, "Well, son, that depends on who wins the battles you will be forced to fight."[7]

Chapter 9

So Where Do We Go From Here?

What are the situations of your life that are not working for you? And what are the situations of your life that are working for you as a male? As I raise this question in terms of *Growing Up Male in America*, I realize that it is not just a national attitude or a social definition of masculinity, or a description of gender role that will satisfy the conservative, fundamental, evangelistic Christians. It is a matter, however, of places where you can heal. Christianity, for example, permeates the very fabric of our society, and, as a result, this impact has to be considered as an influential part of growing up male in America. The divinity of the Biblical scriptures or the promise of these scriptures is for every male, as well as every woman.

Iyanla Vanzant, author of *Up From Here, Reclaiming the Male Spirit,* declares,

> One concept of healing is that it's the application of love to the wounded places, the places where there is darkness or ignorance . . . These places require infinite amounts of love. When they [American males] get that love—when we learn to take the power and strength of our own love and apply it to those internal places . . . the places of injury, where chipping, cracking, and stretching almost to breaking

has occurred—then healing occurs . . . Love isn't anything that we do; [necessarily] rather, it's who we are and what we are.

Vanzant continues,

> Men in this [American] culture are taught how to live—how to get, to have, and to do all the things they're told represent what a man should be. The job. The house. The family. And let's not forget the car! All of these represent the things a man is supposed to have in order to be acknowledged and accepted.
>
> But what does it really mean to be a man? Depending on who's asked, the answer could be anything from a rich and powerful influential leader of people to a gun-toting, foul-mouthed renegade. To a 90 percent certainty, though, most of the definitions would lean toward *having or doing* a particular thing. Rarely would someone respond that manhood is a *state of being*. No, being a man is generally defined by what a man *does*. Doing is *physical;* it's *action*. For men doing is the defining function of the masculine persona. *Being*, on the other hand, is *spiritual*. It's an inward movement, a consciousness of the natural essence. Few men are taught the true spiritual essence of their masculinity.[1]

T. Walter Herbert, author of *Sexual Violence and American Manhood,* recognizes that the feminist movement of the sixties sought freedom from ingrained habits of subservience that they had come to feel were natural and right. Herbert believes that the women of the sixties freed themselves from themselves: they set their personal stories in an historical context and learned to understand spontaneous impulses as the outcomes of social arrangements. Likewise, T. W. Herbert claims that growing boys internalize models of manhood that shape the landscape on which we take our bearings day by day. Traditions, however, believed to make us men enter the textures of individual experience by stealth and understanding them requires uncovering the reality behind a deceptive façade of behavior. One of these traditions called "Natural manhood" was taken to mean that men are equally entitled to rule over women, who fulfill their "natural" womanhood in subservience. Warrior manhood, in the similar practice of entitlement, visualized women as sexually subservient. Contemporary gang rapes are a horrible example of the social dynamics of a twisted democratic theory in which the warrior manhood is secured through the degradation of women.[2]

Undeniably, there are new forces that seem to have changed the nature of masculinity, and these changes are not the complete story. Actually, modern assumptions about what constitutes masculinity, male behavior, and individual male identity have been gradually created over the last few centuries. As has already been reviewed from an historical perspective, the idea of man/masculine/manly has shifted throughout history in response to the prevailing social and cultural demands. Assumptions, aspirations, and ideals, conscious or unconscious, are as much a part of reality as physiology.[3]

Few authors chasing the history of masculinity or what it means to be a man in America today refer to the spiritual dimension as pointedly as Vanzant does. I have taken various directions as I have referenced historical, social, political, psychological, and personal proposals about the developmental environment that impacts a man into the image that he is supposed to be. None of these theories, philosophies, or perspectives fully satisfy the question, "What does it mean to be a man?" I have met men who look strikingly masculine and then become a disappointment (based on my assumptions) as I become acquainted with them. The reverse is just as true for me. *Where do we go from here?*

Although I did not think so as I first set out to explore and write about this subject very dear to my heart, I have to say that I now believe that the spiritual dimension has as much validity, if not more than all the rest. Along with Vanzant, Phyllis Burke raises questions that are not just typical historic, social, academic discussions. There is a spiritual dimension that plays in any gender question, and she begins to respond to the spiritual integration in her book, *Gender Shock.* The front flap of the cover raised the question,

> At a time when men are staying at home to parent and women are leaving to practice law, medicine, and politics, America is confused and anxious about what differences truly exist between the sexes. To explore one's gender role is to invite chaos, yet the questions persist: in a world of evolving roles for both sexes, how are "masculine" and "feminine" defined? If women and men are created equal, how then do gender differences emerge?[4]

This is not a legal question. It goes beyond that dimension and far into the spiritual dimension where we are afraid to go because the spiritual dimension, as compared to the religious dimension and others, resists being politicized.

For the sake of recollection, let's look back and quickly review to some degree a summary of the directions I have asked you to look into. There are three paragraphs in Phyllis Burke's preface to *Gender Shock* which will do the review in a proficient way. Unlike a fingerprint or DNA which leaves evidence of our presence, genital identification labels us and prescribes our functional and dysfunctional behavior in a society that expects us to accept and to trust its validity. Burke speaks of behavior modification by using the philosophy of "appropriate behavioral reinforcement," which means when you are told often enough and punished often enough, you will get the message—some sooner and some later. I was one of those later ones. This, of course, added to my confusion and to the confusion of a lot of other young boys of which I spoke earlier. She writes,

> Most children are successful at suppressing the unwanted behaviors, if not the feelings. Yet as they grow and try to establish relationships with the opposite sex, reality becomes a split screen arrangement, with each child secretly suppressing the unwanted feelings, while trying to find someone else who will express them for him, for her. They are off on a lifelong journey to find the other half of themselves. They try to build adolescent and adult relationships with each other, but they rarely work, because no one else can ever give us the other half of our identity. They turn to books of gender gurus like Marianne Williamson's *A Woman's Worth* or John Gray's *Men Are From Mars, Women Are From Venus* where they are told that their anxiety over their masculinity or femininity, and their concerns and fears about their relationships with the opposite sex, can be cured by believing that gender roles are innate and natural. [What an absolute farce!] . . . . In this way, the gender gurus offer a rationalization for why relationships do not work . . . In the long run, these gurus intensify the psychic damage caused by forcing all men and all women into the two categories of masculine and feminine, and by implying that if a man feels a "feminine" trait or a woman feels a "masculine" trait, there is something wrong with them, and that they are in denial about their true selves.[5]

To make her point quite clear about the confusion caused by gender gurus, Burke referred to an acquaintance, a Minnesota radio host, who was interviewing her. She reports that while being interviewed, her radio host felt vindicated when Burke explained to her that a person could be a biological woman, with a masculine gender expression, and be heterosexual in her orientation. Burke says that when the Minnesota host looked deep inside herself, following the advice of Williamson and Gray, she did not find a suppressed feminine identity, but a wide range of human traits. Some traits were masculine and some feminine, and all of them properly belonged to her.[6]

About midway in my own career development and my own growing up processes, I was frequently called upon by organizations and particularly government organizations to help primarily male groups gain insight into interpersonal relations. It was believed that the more these male employees, who were hired to serve and protect the public, were aware of self and conscious of acceptable differences in others, the more capable they would be in the performance of their duties. Yes, I even worked with state and local police organizations. Sometimes I believe a change in viewpoints occurred and sometimes a change did not happen.

One of the things I would do by way of introducing the ominous subject of human relations would be to question the audience's perception of themselves. An opening question I would begin with was "Are you all red-blooded, 100% American Males?" Of course they were—as they in unison jumped to their feet to assure me that they certainly were. While they were still on their feet and becoming quiet, I would ask, "Then how did you get here?" The audience seated themselves and became completely quiet. "Well, were you hatched? Or were you born?" Now a few responses were ventured forth, but with uncertainty. "Did you have both a mother and a father? Certainly, you did and I think you ought to have learned in freshman high school biology that it was only one chromosome out of forty-eight that turned you into either a male or a female. If you still don't get it, fellas, nearly one half of you is a contribution from your mother's genes. And it is medically true as well as biologically true; in the formation of the fetus, we all began as females. Yet males, especially, struggle to hide, deny, suppress, and ignore this female contribution in the very core of their being. I know that I did, and I know that most men I know do too."

Perhaps by now you may be saying, "Okay, so open this spiritual window so we can look into this direction." Yes, I understand, but I feel obligated to substantiate this direction as compared to others in a "real" sense. In *Gender Shock*, Burke presents the seeds of gender identity as behavior, appearance, and science. As a result of her research, she has come to believe that gender, sex, and sexuality are three distinct domains.[7]

Incidents and experiences of gender shock are accelerating because there is a current refusal to live a masquerade life of half an identity. A culture revolution is mounting more and more energy, and gender roles are being challenged as seen in the fewer sex-segregated institutions which are held in less and less esteem and the growing acceptance of men as being psychologically and emotionally capable of rearing a girl and/or boy with as much sensitivity as a woman. It was Burke's intention to do more in *Gender Shock* than to just point out problems. She wanted to offer a new path of consideration beyond myths and to encourage the revolution in human identity that can lead to gender independence. Burke suggests that the confusion caused by insistence upon gender identification can be embodied into the concept of a demon, a mythological demon of destruction, confusion, separation, and torment. We are reminded that, in Roman mythology, the demon was an attendant spirit or power which had unusual motivational drive and vitality. The demon was a raw gift of talented energy from the divine, and it often went by the name of or was referred to as "genius." Could it be true that the genius lies dormant within us all, as we shut it out and try to live as *"real men and real women."* I agree with Burke, that the genius is waiting to be acknowledged.[8]

Chapter 10

Let's Go An Old Direction
A Different Way

In the beginning pages of this book, I wanted to describe the confusion of growing up as an American male and, perhaps, after sixty some years of living as an American male, offer some suggestions about how our culture, society, and family life might change to benefit and be more supportive of American males. The reader had to journey through chapters of my personal perception about what was and what happened to me as a middle class American male, and more broadly understand what happens to many American males in the context of our surrounding culture and in the context of our manipulative society that seems to value moralisms as a means of controlling consumerism more than it values healthy human life.

As I poured over a considerable number of volumes or research on American masculinity and the many issues impacting what the definition of a male is supposed to look like and what a male is supposed to act like, I came to realize that most of the research isolated masculinity as gender behavior, as body appearance, as test levels of competitiveness, as performers of accomplishment, as heroes of strength and bravery, as those who inherit the traditional social values, which they are expected to carry on no matter how painful, no matter how purposeless, no matter how worthless the traditional value may cause them to feel.

Admittedly, I struggled writing with a bias in my mind and that bias and/or question was "Could masculinity be defined spiritually?" This direction of research into the spiritual nature of maleness was unlikely to even be considered by the authors I had read until I examined what Iyanla Vanzant and Phyllis Burke had to say. As I said in the previous chapter, I now believe that the creating spirit is as much a valid dimension of gender identity as any other means of theorizing. Perhaps there are those who believe only in the dimensions of mind and body to explain the essence of masculinity, but I am one of those males who believes that I am mind, body and *spirit*.

Is a person who is homosexual somehow less of a whole person than a person who is heterosexual? Are stay-at-home dads who are supported by professional wives not real males? Are interior decorators, fashion designers, and male beauticians less masculine than athletes? When men cross occupational lines into traditionally female professions, are they less masculine? What assumptions are in play? And just how valid are those assumptions? If we believe at all in the *great creative source of life* (why not a synonym for God?), then we all share the same eventuating spirit that brings all things from nonexistence into existence. Most scientists will agree that energy is a process of exchanging information. The more information exchanged the higher level of energy and the more energy generated the greater possibility of creative change. The point is that we all emerge from the same process of coming into being. What turns us into self-conscious, egotistical judges of how to determine what is right and wrong? It is our attitudes which most probably are supported by unfounded assumptions. Who was it that taught me that what keeps us from the reality of truth is mankind's own intellectual allusions?

Instead of teaching the principles of peace and harmony with all gifts of the creative spirit, we teach separateness, unkindness, disrespect, selfishness, greed, shame, and guilt. Jeffrey Marx, author of *Season of Life*, writes about his relationship with Joe Ehrmann, former NFL football star, who is a former captain of the Baltimore Colts and now an ordained minister. In one of the many dialogues throughout the book, Joe said,

> Masculinity, first and foremost, ought to be defined in terms of relationships. It ought to be taught in terms of the capacity to *love* and to *be loved*. If you look over your life at the end of it . . . life wouldn't be measured in terms of success based on what you've

acquired or achieved or what you own. The only thing that's really going to matter is the relationships that you had.[1]

And again, further along in the book, the author, J. Marx, asks Joe Ehrmann a hypothetical question,

> How would you explain your own definition of what it means to be a man? "It's about relationships and a cause," Joe said, "Simple as that. What's a man created to do? . . . I think you try to speak into people's real lives, . . . Some men just grab hold of it. Something I say might help them get connected to the pain in their lives. They might be ready for something new and different. But I don't ever know when it's really going to kick in for someone . . . But I do know this, it's really soul work. Something has to grab you in your soul. I don't think it's just cognitive."[2]

As J. Marx continued in dialogue with Joe Ehrmann, the definition of what it means to be a man in relationships became more explicit. Joe told Marx,

> Most of us have a huge father pain somewhere deep down inside, a huge father longing . . . Because we have never been accepted, never been embraced the way we need to be . . . [There is a common condition—known to psychologists as normative male *alexithymia*—that goes a long way in explaining why many men struggle with relationships. The word *alexithymia* has Greek roots. It means the inability to put emotions into words. As described by psychologist Ronald F. Levant, who has written extensively on masculinity, "Normative *alexithymia* is] a predictable result of the male gender role socialization process. Specifically, it is a result of boys being socialized to restrict the expression of their vulnerable and caring/connection emotions and to be emotionally stoic."[3]

It is generally known that infant boys, when compared to infant girls, begin life more tuned into emotional expression. Boys who are between six months and two years of age are startled more easily and are more easily excitable. Infant boys cry sooner when frustrated and shift moods more quickly than infant girls. It is observable, however, that by the age of two boys are beginning to suppress their emotional responses. Is it any wonder that men live most of their emotional lives in pseudo-community? For many American males an authentic relationship with women and/or men becomes a reach too far. Because of their confusion men devote a great deal of time and effort to their cosmetic armor that hides and protects and limits access to their authentic self.

Isn't it amazing that our free American society that champions human rights begins at a male's stage of infancy to teach suppressive behavior in terms of mind and body? Perhaps, a considerable number of American males who are born into Christian families in America will have little exposure to the meaning of their spiritual nature. It is doubtful, nevertheless, that any remarkable difference will be made to challenge the cultural moralisms that provide American male armor before the age of three.

Two of America's leading child psychologists, Dan Kindlon, Ph.D., and Michael Thompson, Ph.D., willingly offer society what knowledge that they have accumulated over thirty-five years of combined experience in research and therapy with boys and their families. One does not have to become too absorbed into these authors' research before realizing that they believe that American males can become whole persons in body, mind, and spirit, when American culture and socialization processes provide a safe environment in which that individual development can happen. Kindlon and Thompson share seven points that they believe have the potential to transform, nurture, and protect the emotional life of our American males.

The seven points are as follows:

1. Give boys permission to have an internal life, approval for the full range of human emotions, and help in developing an emotional vocabulary so that they may better understand themselves and communicate more effectively with others.
2. Recognize and accept the high activity level of boys and give them safe boy places to express it.
3. Talk to boys in their language—in a way that honors their pride and their masculinity. Be direct with them; use them as consultants and problem solvers.
4. Teach boys that emotion courage is courage, and that courage and empathy are the sources of real strength in life.
5. Use discipline to build character and conscience, not enemies.
6. Model a manhood of emotional attachment.
7. Teach boys that there are many ways to be a man.[4]

In the third chapter of *Smart Boys* by Barbara A. Kerr, Ph.D., and Sanford J. Cohn, Ph.D, the authors quote from *Real Boys' Voices* by William Pollack

> First, there are the ideas that boys carry with them—the code of boys' culture. The Boy Code, as Pollack calls it, is a type of straightjacket for boys, cruelly restricting their emotions and behaviors. Its first imperative is to be "The Sturdy Oak": stoic, stable, and independent. Boys are never to show weakness, they cannot have moods, and they must never depend on anyone for help. The second imperative is to "Give 'em Hell!: that is they should engage in risky, daring behavior and should act tough and macho at all times. The third is "Big Wheel," namely that males must attain status, dominance, and power . . . The fourth is "No Sissy Stuff": males must never show empathy or demonstrate emotional responses to another. This one [this aspect of the code] says Pollack, may be the most crippling, because it requires that boys submerge all human qualities previously, though mistakenly, attributed to females only.[5]

A further perspective that Pollack offers resurfaced many images of my childhood. Pollack says, "Parents worry if their boy is not masculine and often try to search for ways of making him more of a man." This belief about boys who did not appear to be as masculine as expected in their behavior caused immediate suspect and labeling as sissy or homosexual. It was certainly true in my grade school days, and my peers saw me as a neighborhood bully. Eventually, I realized I did not have to be a bully to be accepted. I remember the confusion and the fear. I did not want to be suspect, and yet I was quite uncomfortable being a bully. It has struck me that I do not remember my female cousins ever being punished or receiving harsh treatment because they were "tom boys." It appears that society regards boys to be destructive to the foundations of culture when left to themselves.

As I have been working on this chapter, a visiting friend became rather anxious to read some of what I had written. I handed him the pages I had just written on this particular chapter. He understood the emphasis that I placed on relationships and then made a comment about my anger relative to the content of the book. He made a comment about the research I had done, but there was no identification with the theme of the content. There was nothing for him to own or connect to as a male growing up in America. I suppose this reaction of denial will be true for those males who grew up with everything fitting into place. For the most part, his emotional pain was limited to ending a relationship with a married woman when he was young and single and when his parents died. He has a few other significant emotional responses, but otherwise his sociable armor is well in place. He is not in touch with his fellow men who have been downsized, men who have been groomed for traditional roles in society and now the roles no longer exist, or men who have been gang members seeking their manhood. This is what Susan Faludi, a well-known feminist author, exposes in her book about the anger of American men. In her book, *Stiffed: The Betrayal of the American Man*, many of the men are sad and angry. What changes happened in the last thirty years began happening to men sixty years ago, and by the age of three years the eventual matrix of betrayal was set to happen.

> Like most human attributes, masculinity is complexly determined and is not the result of a single substance [like testosterone]. Masculinity is the result of a wide variety of both internal and external forces. As such, it is just as open to interpretation as it is to shaping.[6]

The interpretation of masculinity spreads across all of the individual cultures of the world. And yet, there is a common bond, and that bond is the spirit of man. The spirit tries and tries to unite each individual man within himself in the same way the spirit connects mankind throughout the world. Relationships reach across boundaries and borders and bind us in alliances of the spirit. Grasp the following paragraph and hang on to its truthful facts:

> People who are more balanced in masculine and feminine characteristics seem to have more flexibility in living their lives. Two decades of research on androgyny—a psychological stance that incorporates the strengths of both masculinity and femininity—show it to be associated with psychological health, creativity, better social functioning, and lower rates of substance abuse. (Bem, 1999) The best literature on masculinity does not advise a return to a macho world in which men dominate, compete, and make all the decisions, but rather advises a society in which males are able to be emotionally responsive, nurturing, and compassionate as well.[7]

In contrast to the psychological and philosophical direction of androgyny, Lisa Wilson presents the "Domestic Life of Men in Colonial New England" in her book, *Ye Heart A Man*. The domestic life of men was a lock step pattern of existence. She writes:

> A man operated in the domestic world as a key member of an interdependent family. A man's sense of self came from performing adequately in his family and in his community. "Usefulness" in the domestic realm defined an adult male. Independence was merely a temporary stage that freed him from the subordination of childhood and allowed him to begin a family of his own. Autonomy was not the goal, in fact it was quickly ameliorated by marriage. Likewise, dependency or "uselessness" was to be avoided at all costs. A kind of relational and fluctuating patriarchal power framed the domestic lives of these good men . . . .
>
> By the nineteenth century, men looked to the world outside their families and immediate communities for self-definition. Domestic concerns gave way to public ones. Men were consigned to the public sphere and women to the private. Men competed with one another in this public domain for status and resources. Usefulness became less valued than individual achievement. Such men became detached from the colonial emphasis on service to family and community that the successful and admired were dubbed "self-made."[8]

There is an apparent transformation of male sexuality and the definition of masculinity that must be taken into account before moving on to a *different* way. The military man and virtue of being a warrior has formulated an elemental role from Middle Age chivalry to worldwide terrorism. Leo Braudy, author of *From Chivalry to Terrorism*, has traced the changes in perceptions of masculinity/sexuality through the historical attitudes of military confrontations. In addition, Braudy gathered influencing meaning from the historical phases of literature and art regarding male sexuality. He demonstrates how crucial points in history, such as various inventions or discoveries transformed the civilized world and transformed concepts of masculinity. Braudy believes that it is the redeveloped warriors masculinity that is at the heart of the exaggerated preachments of the Islamic terrorists. For the warrior terrorists there has to be an absolute separation between male and female characteristics, which was true for Hitler and the Nazi movement for example. It is suggested that the war against terrorism today is not so much a war about territory and resources as it is a war motif about how men should act. What Braudy has written strongly suggests that masculinity is not simply a matter of innate behavior, but is a matter of adaptability, modification, and active responsiveness to circumstantial conditions.[9]

The male image and the content of the definition of masculinity have been polarized, as has been described throughout this book. In the 1990's two more polarizations occurred. "Carol Gilligan is probably the intellectual mainstay of the *sensitive man movement*," says Mark O'Connell, author of The *Good Father*. He continues to explain what Gilligan means in terms of male development into a sensitive human being:

> Gilligan tells us that boys suffer from a host of psychological liabilities, primary among them an intolerance of feelings and vulnerability, along with an incapacity to form meaningful relationships. She writes: "If boys in early childhood resist the break between the inner and outer worlds, they are resisting an initiation into masculinity or manhood as it is defined and established in cultures that value or valorize heroism, honor, war, competition—the culture of the warrior, the economy of capitalism . . . To be a real man in such a culture means to be able to hurt without feeling hurt, to separate without feeling sadness or loss, and then to inflict hurt or separation on others.[10]

The movement for "the sensitive man" has an impressive list of supporters:

The Men They Will Become: The Nature and Nurture of Male Character, by Eli Newberger
I Don't Want to Talk About It: Overcoming the Secret Legacy of Male Depression, by Terrence Real
The Courage to Raise Good Men: You Don't Have to Sever the Bond with Your Son to Help Him Become a Man, by Olga Silverstein and Beth Rashbaum
Real Boys: Rescuing Our Sons from the Myths of Boyhood, by William Pollack
Masculinity Reconstructed: Changing the Rules of Manhood, by Ron Levant
Raising Cain: Protecting the Emotional Life of Boys, by Dan Kindlon and Michael Thompson
Stiffed: The Betrayal of the American Man, by Susan Faludi
Manhood in America: A Cultural History, by Michael Kimmel

I believe this movement and its supporters have done a much-needed service for the benefit of many American males. However, I do not believe there is a panacea in any of the theories that have been presented.

> Constructs such as masculinity derive their meaning from, among other influences, the dialectical relationship that exists between culture and biology. [The sensitive man movement] . . . shifts rapidly. Culture-based fluctuations in our sense of who we are occur in the space of ten year intervals, sometimes even more frequently. [The Real Man movement] based on biology shifts more glacially. Changes in the biological underpinnings of selfhood become evident only over the course of many generations. While the pace of each of these [movements] and their effects are different, both simultaneously exert a powerful influence on our sense of identity . . . the sensitive man movement errs by overvaluing the influence of culture while failing to recognize the powerful, unremitting impact of biology. The result? It offers a naively prescriptive view of what it believes men should be, while failing to ally that view with a realistic appreciation of what men are.[11]

It is understandable that the sensitive man movement would instigate a counter movement like the real man movement. All around us [in the mass media] . . . and all around our children, there are images of pumped-up alternatives to the sensitive man; however, these pop-culture manifestations of manliness are less defined by stoicism, competition, and aggression than by beer-swilling, backslapping, and obsessions with large breasts (both men's and women's).

As a part of the counter-reaction to the feminists support of the sensitive man, there is a plethora of publications and internet ads for bigger muscles, bigger penises, and ever more masculinity-inflating sexual conquests. Anti-feminists have not remained silent. There are authors like Richard Doyle, who wrote *The Rape of the Male,* in which he writes, "Feminist women are *would-be castrators with a knee-jerk, obsessive aversion to anything male.*" In *The Failure of Feminism,* journalist Nicholas Davidson argues that, "Feminists demand unnatural contortions from men, such as *trying not to feel aggressiveness of dominance toward a woman when making love to her.*"[12]

There is much more to be said on each side of this debate to be sure, and some of the issues are new perspectives and some have been around since the turn of the century and before. Some useful truths have emerged, and some exaggerations have taken on new imagery, and some myths have been demythologized, and the American male realizes, that in order to survive, he must be authentic. He must be mind, body, and SPIRIT. Steroids, religious dogma, stressful ideology, and suppression are not healthy for the spirit of man which is living in all of us.

Perhaps it was in my later years of high school and college that I began to experience some clarity about by idealistic self. I began to understand that the spirit of the ideal American male could be exemplified in the Constitution of the United States. I began to understand that the *amber waves of grain and the alabaster cities' gleam* symbolized the spirited vision of American men, and when I hear the lyrics *still wave over the land of the free and the home of the brave*—my heart swells with a pilgrim's spirit of great visualizations. Gradually, I understood that the spirit of justice is the face of God, and not just some concept of fairness that can be politicized into a selfish gain. The spirit of justice is often manipulated by the majority. The spirit I am talking about inspires us to a conviction of greater good in each of us and for our fellowman. I am not blinded by patriotic religiosity or the contradictory assumptions of organized religion represented by various denominations of Christianity. It is ironic, I know, to recommend the unifying force between mind and body as spirit, especially when the Judeo-Christian tradition is struggling to understand masculinity and equality with gay/lesbian believers.

The spirit that unifies my body and my mind is the spirit that gives voice to this realization,

> You are all sons of God through faith in Christ Jesus, for all of you who were baptized into Christ have clothed yourselves with Christ. There is neither Jew nor Greek, slave nor free, male nor female, for you are all one in Christ Jesus (NIV)

To me this suggests that we are all one despite our individual differences of race, sex, financial levels, or whether some are heterosexual or homosexual. It is fear that captivates and oppresses men and causes confusion about the boy code, which says nothing about the spirit. The greater good of men's spirit advocates and protects the basic human rights of all individuals—excluding no one, at least this is the intent.

Homophobic attitudes hold both the gay and straight men as prisoners. Both suffer, although it may be in different ways. Listen to this promise of being liberated:

> The Spirit of the Lord is on me, because he has anointed me to preach good news to the poor. He has sent me to proclaim freedom for the prisoners and recovery of sight for the blind, to release the oppressed, to proclaim the year of the Lord's favor. (NIV)

It truly amazes me that well-meaning Christians resist opening up their church polity to allow for the ordination of avowed homosexual persons when the great prophets of the Old Testament and the Gospels do not speak about gay/lesbian orientation.[13]

Some say to me that it is only a matter of time and the divided men will find a way to come together individually and as an entire population. It is suggested that change takes time and I wonder how long American males will have to wait when I review how many changes have taken place in my lifetime. My generation has incorporated a great many things since birth, such as:

> Television, polio shots, frozen food, Xerox, plastics, contact lenses, Frisbees, and the Pill. Recall that many of us were born before credit cards, split atoms, laser beams, and ballpoint pens; before panty hose, dishwashers, and before electric blankets, air conditioners, drip dry clothes, and before people walked on the moon. Your life has changed, and without being afraid, you lived before you heard of FM radios, tape decks, electronic typewriters, artificial hearts, word processors, CDs, yogurt, and guys wearing earrings. You lived at a time when hardware meant hardware and software wasn't even a word. You can recall when a chip meant a piece of wood, when grass was mowed with a push mower, Coke was a cold drink, and pot was something you cooked in.[14]

Why is it so difficult to acknowledge the rights of everyone? While all men are affected by stereotypic ideas of masculinity, currently homosexual men are receiving much more negative attention. The word *homosexuality* is a relatively new word, and not actually a biblical one. Meanings get fixed by words. New meanings can produce new words, but not if unintended meanings are read into them. The term *homosexuality* or *homosexual* was not adapted into the English language from German until 1892. The implications of this understanding have far reaching questions regarding biblical support for condemnation of homosexual relationships. George R. Edwards, professor and an impressive biblical scholar at Louisville Presbyterian theological Seminary, has accumulated such weighty research that anyone attempting to comment on views of masculinity and/or homosexuality based on biblical scholarship cannot ignore his work, *Gay and Lesbian Liberation: A Biblical Perspective.* Paul's letters in the New Testament are often misinterpreted in today's modern life situations, especially Romans and Corinthians. However, Edwards explains the broader meaning of the New Testament word *agape`* as the expression of evangelical love by which the only Unique Son of God was sent for human deliverance. God's love for the world becomes in evangelical belief the distinctive element in the formation of all human loves. Our moral instruction is to love God and to love our neighbor, whoever and however he may be. And in First John 4:4-19, we are informed that God is love and the dying of His Son transforms human love. The love commandment implies that we are to carry *agape`* into the total area of human experience.[14]

> The Fruit of the Spirit is love, joy, peace, patience, kindness, goodness, faithfulness, gentleness, and self-control. Against such things there is no law. Those who belong to Christ Jesus have crucified the sinful nature with its passion and desires. Since we live by the Spirit, let us keep step with the Spirit. (NIV)

According to Edwards it is the constancy of God's love shown in Christ that gives to human love—including sexual love—its quality as history in which sexuality becomes a renewal for the acceptance of another and the willingness to be transformed for the sake of the other.

My brothers, we are liberated, we are freed by the spirit in all of us. We no longer have to be a confused dichotomy of mind and body, but we can experience wholeness in and through spirit. "Who shall separate us from the love of Christ?" (NIV, Romans 8:35)

Now, perhaps, as the reader you are saying or thinking to yourself, "Yes, but what if I am not a particularly religious believer and certainly not a believer in organized religion of any kind, and surely not Christianity." That stance is fine. When I talk about theorizing in terms of the spiritual nature of human beings, I am not being exclusively "Christian" in my approach to masculinity.

The spiritual nature of being a man involves what he believes, i.e. the spirit of human rights, the spirit of freedom, the spirit of justice, and so on. Sam Harris, in his book *The End of Faith*, says:

> A belief is a lever that once pulled moves almost everything in a person's life. Are you a scientist? A liberal? A racist? These are merely species of belief in action. Your beliefs define your vision of the world; they dictate your behavior; they determine your emotional responses to other human beings.[16]

Is this the turn key? Is this the pivotal point of figuring out our maleness and all the stereotypic beliefs about our behavior? I would like to believe that there is a spirit of charity that lifts us above and allows us to imagine the ideal and make it work like the "City of Brotherly Love." It is not reality yet, but the community of Philadelphia keeps working on it. Like in communities that are ravaged by earthquakes, hurricanes, floods, or fires, people help other people and by pulling together and working together they believe they can make a difference and they do.

> Each and every man can make a difference by viewing each other capable man as "good enough" to think, to feel, to believe, to accept, to be.

Acknowledgements

Chapter 1

1. From FIRE IN THE BELLY by Sam Keen. New York:,copyright 1991. Used with permission from Bantam Books.

Chapter 3

1. *Ibid.*
2. Reprinted with the permission of Scribner, an imprint of Simon and Schuster Adult Publishing Group, from I DO NOT WANT TO TALK ABOUT IT: OVERCOMING THE SECRET LEGACY OF MALE DEPRESSION by Terrence Real. Copyright 1997 by Terry Real. All rights reserved. P. 123.
3. *Ibid.*
4. *Ibid.*
5. *Ibid.*
6. *Ibid.*, 127-128.

Chapter 4

1. From MEN THEY WILL BECOME: THE NATURE AND NURTURE OF MALE CHARACTER by Eli Newberger. Reprinted by permission of Da Capo Press, a member of the Perseus Books Group, 1999. P. 4.
2. *Ibid., p. 8.*
3. *Ibid., p. 13.*

4. *Ibid, p. 15*
5. Ibid., 17.

Chapter 5

1. From THE SECRET LIFE OF MEN by Steve Biddulph. Copyright 2003. Appears by permission of the publisher, Marlowe, A Division of Avalon Publishing Group, Inc. P. 139.

Chapter 6

1. *Ibid., p. 3*
2. *Ibid. p. 3*
3. From "Masculinity Under Fire" by John Ibson in LOOKING AT LIFE MAGAZINE, Edited by Erika Doss. Published by Smithsonian Institution Press, 2001. P. 181.
4. *Ibid., p. 181.*
5. *Ibid., p. 180.*
6. *Ibid.,* p. 182.
7. *Ibid.* p. 183
8. *Ibid., pp. 185-189.*
9. *Ibid., p. 190.*
10. *Ibid., 190.*
11. *Ibid., 190.*
12. *Ibid., 191.*
13. *Ibid., 192*
14. *Ibid. 193-4*
15. Reprinted with permission by Dr. Matthew McKay, Ph.D. and Patrick Fanning. BEING A MAN: A GUIDE TO THE NEW MASCULINITY by Patrick Fanning and Matthew McKay, Ph.D. New Harbinger Publications, 1993. Pp. 107-108.

Chapter 7

1. Karamargin, CJ, P BI, *Arizona Daily Star, Feb. 15, 2004.*
2. From THE MASCULINE MYSTIQUE by Andrew Kimbrell, copyright 1995 by Andrew Kimbrell. Used by permission of Ballantine Books, a division of Random House, Inc.

Chapter 8

1. From CASTRATION: AN ABBREVIATED HISTORY OF WESTERN MANHOOD by Gary Taylor. Copyright 2000. Reproduced by permission of Routledge/Taylor & Francis Group.
LLC. P. 11.
2. *Ibid., pp. 12-13*
3. *Ibid., p. 13.*
4. *Ibid. p. 15.*
5. *Ibid., p. 29-30*
6. *Ibid., p. 33-78*
7. *Ibid., p. 233.*

Chapter 9

1. From UP FROM HERE: RECLAIMING THE MALE SPIRIT by Iyanla Vanzant. Copyright 2002 by Iyanla Vanzant. Reprinted by permission of HarperCollins Publishers. Pp. 3-4.
2. Reprinted by permission of the publisher from SEXUAL VIOLENCE AND AMERICAN MANHOOD by T. Walter Herbert, Cambridge, Mass.: Harvard University Press, Copyright 2002 by the President and Fellows of Harvard College. P. 61.
3. From GENDER SHOCK by Phyllis Burke, copyright 1996 by Phyllis Burke. Used by permission of Doubleday, a division of Random House, Inc. Front Cover.
4. *Ibid. p. xxi.*
5. *Ibid., p. xxiii*
6. *Ibid., p. xxiv-xxv.*
7. *Ibid., p. xxiv-xxv.*

Chapter 10

1. Reprinted with the permission of Simon & Schuster Adult Publishing Group, from SEASON OF LIFE: A FOOTBALL STAR, A BOY, A JOURNEY TO MANHOOD by Jeffrey Marx. Copyright 2003 by Jeffrey Marx. All rights reserved. P. 36.
2. *Ibid., pp.99-100.*
3. *Ibid., pp. 100-101.*

4. From REAL BOYS' VOICES by William Pollack, copyright 2000 by William Pollack. Used by permission of Random House, Inc.

5. *Ibid.*

6. From SMART BOYS: TALENT, MANHOOD, AND THE SEARCH FOR MEANING by Barbara A. Kerr and Sanford J. Cohn. Copyright 2001 by Kerr and Cohn. Used with permission of Great Potential Press. p. 89.

7. *Ibid., p. 96.*

8. From YE HEART OF MAN: THE DOMESTIC LIFE OF MEN IN COLONIAL ENGLAND by Lisa Wilson, copyright 1999 by Lisa Wilson. Used by permission of Yale University Press. Page 188.

9. From FROM CHIVALRY TO TERRORISM by Leo Braudy. Alfred A. Knoopf, 2003.

10. Reprinted with the permission of Scribner, an imprint of Simon & Schuster Adult Publishing Group, from THE GOOD FATHER: ON MEN, MASCUJLINITY, AND LIFE IN THE FAMILY by Mark O'Connell, Ph.D. Copyright 2005 by Mark O'Connell, Ph.D. All rights reserved. Pp. 23-24.

11. *Ibid., pp. 31-32.*

12. *Ibid., p. 33.*

13. Dr. John Ross, sermon "It Ain't Sitting Still" February 13, 2005, Valley Presbyterian Church, Green Valley, AZ.

14. From THE END OF FAITH: RELIGION, TERROR, AND THE FUTURE OF REASON by Sam Harris, copyright 2005 by Sam Harris. Used with permission of WW Norton & Company.